HOSTILE
FIRE

**The Life & Death
of First Lieutenant
Sharon Lane**

Also by the author. . .

In Honored Glory
Washington in Focus
Failing Grades

HOSTILE FIRE

The Life & Death
of First Lieutenant
Sharon Lane

PHILIP BIGLER

VANDAMERE
PRESS

Published by
Vandamere Press
A Division of AB Associates
P.O. Box 5243
Arlington, VA 22205

Dedicated to
Cdr. Charles E. Bigler, USNR (ret.)
and to the Memory of
Bernice R. Bigler

ACKNOWLEDGMENTS

In the summer of 1991, I first contacted Mrs. Kay Lane to discuss the possibilities of writing a book about her daughter, Sharon. At that time, she invited me to Canton where we first met later that October. Given the anticipated nature and scope of the project, I told her that I estimated the research and writing of the book would take approximately three years. It ended up taking four.

Over the ensuing years, I had several other opportunities to visit with Mrs. Lane. She gave me complete access to Sharon's extensive personal correspondence along with many other related items. It was quickly apparent to me that Sharon was a prolific and gifted writer. Indeed, during her short six weeks in Vietnam, she wrote 14 letters home. Additionally, during her 10 months at Fitzsimons Hospital she wrote 31 letters and 8 more during basic training at Fort Sam Houston. These letters provide the basis for much of what is recounted here and reflect Sharon's own perspective and view of events. I am indebted to Mrs. Lane for all of her help and assistance during this project. It remains my fondest hope that this finished work will ultimately pay tribute to Sharon and honor her life.

I have had the privilege to meet and interview many remarkable people over these past four years. Larry Hines, who was with the SRAO program at Chu Lai, provided much of the early background on the hospital compound, the war, and the immediate aftermath of the tragic rocket attack of June 8, 1969. Amy Lazar, the Red Cross social worker assigned to the 312th, provided me with a copy of her personal log book, a resource that proved to be a remarkably detailed and specific chronology of the events of 1969. Her support, encouragement, and suggestions were invaluable and much appreciated. On several occasions, I met with Colonel Jack Medlin in Winston-Salem, North Carolina. Jack explained the many details of the 312th's 1968 mobilization and deployment and shared with me his excellent collection of personal photographs. Colonel Pauline Hester, likewise, was a wonderful resource on the unit's subsequent operations in Vietnam and the role of American nurses. I would also like to express my sincere thanks to Mary and Bill Smith for their gracious hospitality and for the vast amount of information they provided during my visit to their home in Ohio. Special thanks also to Lieutenant Colonel Leta Menton who read the final manuscript for accuracy and gave her time and support to the eventual publication of *Hostile Fire*. Many thanks also to the following people who contributed their experiences, memories, expertise, and knowledge: Marilyn Becker, Dwight Bellamy, Rick Castilo, Penny Divito, Fred Fisher, Roger Ford, Marilyn Genz, Sylvia Holland, Jennifer Keen, Patricia Kowal, Gary Leiser, Mary Jo Lobianco, Elizabeth Norman, Warwick Palmer, Cannon Sample, Doris Sheets, Paul Stephanus, and Matt Sullivan.

Dr. Michael Carey, one of the 312th Evacuation Hospital's neurosurgeons, deserves special recognition. I had the privilege to meet with him at his home in New Orleans in February, 1995 and at that time he provided me with countless photographs of the hospital compound along with an enormous amount of factual information. Moreover, he selflessly devoted many hours to carefully reading, evaluating, and editing the manuscript for clarity and accuracy. His efforts have greatly improved and enhanced this final version.

Several of my students have also assisted me over the last few years. I would like to especially thank and recognize four very special and gifted young ladies: Bridget Johnson, Candace Miller, Mandy Neville, and Maureen Ryan. Several of my colleagues, friends, and fellow educators assisted with the final proofreading and indexing: Charlotte Bruce, Fran Pettigrew, Ghislaine Tulou, Philip Walsh, and Wende Walsh. These dedicated and exceptional teachers respresent all that is good and right in American education. I would also like to thank my publisher at Vandamere Press, Art Brown, for his continuing support and encouragement. Likewise, my deepest appreciation to my editor, Pat·Berger, for her usual exceptional work. My wife, Linda, remains my closest partner and a constant source of inspiration. Her perseverance prove crucial.

To these and all of the others who have helped make this book a reality, I would like to express my continuing thanks and gratitude.

TABLE OF CONTENTS

HOSTILE FIRE

**The Life & Death
of First Lieutenant
Sharon Lane**

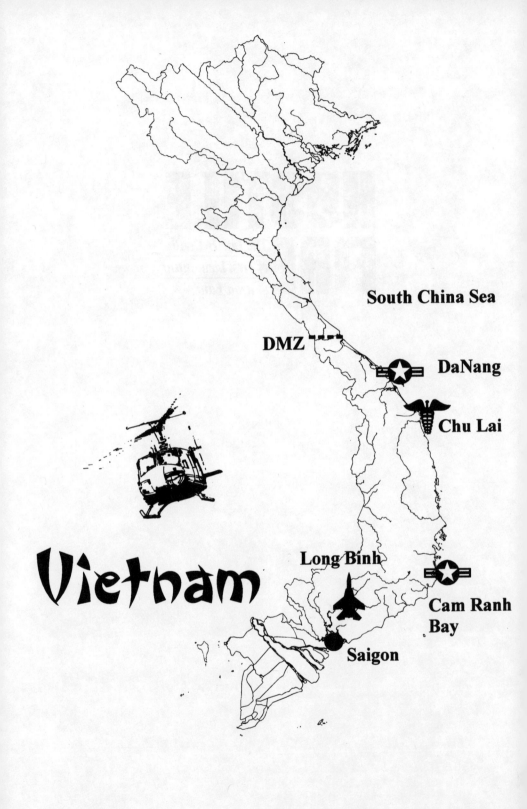

South China Sea

DMZ

DaNang

Chu Lai

Long Binh

Vietnam

Cam Ranh
Bay

Saigon

1

Incoming at Dawn

"Army Nurse Killed in War"

—Washington *Star* (June 1969)

June 8, 1969—The waning crescent moon was directly overhead, but its scant light did little to pierce the darkness that still shrouded the countryside of Quang Tin Province. In the distance, the lights of the American military compound at Chu Lai cast a silver glow. The massive complex of over 10,000 soldiers, headquarters to the Americal Division and the site of the 312th Evacuation Hospital, showed few signs of life during these predawn hours. Only an occasional pair of F-4 Phantoms from the adjacent Marine airfield broke the silence with the deafening roar of their after-burners while their orange flames briefly scarred the night before the jets quickly disappeared on some unknown mission. From above the American compound, a lone Huey helicopter was perpetually circling, dropping its cargo of flares. Each slowly floated back down to earth suspended by a small parachute while briefly illuminating the immediate area in a ghostly, brownish-orange glow before finally being snuffed out by the darkness.

Directly behind the military base was the South China Sea which was bordered by a beautiful, white sand beach. In less troubled times, the region would have been a favored fishing site for Vietnamese peasants in their distinctive round, basket boats but in 1969, there was barbed wire, sand-bagged bunkers, and apprehensive guards peering into the darkness. No American ever ventured out for a cool evening swim or even a solitary walk along the beach out of fear of being mistaken for a Viet Cong (VC) infiltrator.

The night had brought some welcome respite from the cruel, oppressive June heat. A cool ocean breeze was blowing that made sleep possible, but the pale streaks of sunlight now visible along the eastern horizon warned ominously that a new day in Vietnam was about to begin.

Oblivious to all of this was a small platoon of PAVN (People's Army of Vietnam) soldiers from the 3d Regiment, 2d NVA Division. They were lean from meager rations and hardened by months of battle. In their short lifetimes, these soldiers had experienced only war—first against the French colonists followed by war against President Ngo Dinh Diem and now against the Americans. This latest of enemies had proven to be a formidable foe with a force of over 543,000 soldiers in Vietnam. The Americans were brave men and well-equipped for modern warfare with a vast array of weapons that produced awesome firepower. In virtually every battle, the North Vietnamese could expect to be outgunned and face overwhelming technological superiority. Still, the massive Tet Offensive launched the previous year, although a major military defeat, had subsequently proven to be a political success. Five South Vietnamese cities and over 150 towns were simultaneously assaulted by 84,000 communist troops. Despite incredible losses and the disruption of the entire Viet Cong infrastructure, the lasting impact of Tet had been to turn the American people against the war in ever-increasing numbers. Indeed, the offensive had fundamentally changed the Vietnam War. It was no longer being fought solely in the rice paddies of the Mekong, in the triple canopied jungles, or even here along the beaches of the coastal plains. No, the war was instead being waged daily in the living rooms of the American people with television an unwitting ally of the Communist forces by daily beaming back horrific pictures of young, dead American teenagers. With each casualty, morale in the United States steadily declined and the nation's political will to persevere in Vietnam seemed to weaken.

In just the previous two days, heavy fighting throughout Vietnam had cost the lives of an additional 100 American troops, swelling the total American casualties in the war to near 34,000. The fighting had been carefully orchestrated to coincide with the ongoing summit meeting being held that very day on Midway Island between President Richard M. Nixon and South Vietnamese President Nguyen Van Thieu. This distant island site had been carefully selected by American diplomats in an effort to avoid a disrupting embarrassment caused by antiwar demonstrators who were omnipresent in the United States. President Nixon intended to use the forum to formally announce the first significant American troop withdrawals as part of his new program to "Vietnamize" the war. In reality, he was opening the floodgates of withdrawal, a process that once initiated could never be stopped. For the North Vietnamese, it meant that their strategy of prolonged struggle would eventually triumph and that victory over the South Vietnamese would someday be achieved. It was only a distant hope, though, that their 79-year old revolutionary leader, Ho Chi Minh, would live to see it.

The geopolitical implications of the war were of little concern to this small PAVN detachment. They had more immediate and pressing concerns. Their orders called for them to launch a dawn attack against the American military complex at Chu Lai by firing a cluster of Soviet-built rockets against the installation. It had proven to be an arduous assignment.

For much of the night, the PAVN soldiers had carefully eluded American patrols, a task that was further complicated by their bulky cargo. Still, they successfully reached their destination undetected, just a few miles away from the heavily guarded American perimeter surrounding Chu Lai. For almost two hours, the platoon had been digging furiously in the soft, granular soil, trenching a primitive pit that would serve as the launching platform for their rockets, while a sister squad made similar preparations some distance away. Sticks and bamboo were strategically positioned to provide support for the weapons and aim them toward their target.

The Soviet 122-mm rocket was a formidable weapon. Originally designed for use against massed NATO forces in Europe, it was first deployed in 1964. Ideally, the rockets were fired from flatbed trucks equipped with up to 40 launch tubes, an arrangement providing fearsome firepower that could quickly ravage opposing troops. Each missile was equipped with a 41-pound warhead composed of a lethal combination of TNT and aluminum, which, upon detonation, spewed forth hundreds of pieces of deadly shrapnel over a large radius. Thus, the Soviets had sardonically christened the rocket *grad* (hail).

Under ideal conditions, the rockets were fairly accurate weapons, but this required stable launch tubes and traditional battlefields. The North Vietnamese army rarely fought under such circumstances and, as a result, they were forced to adapt and modify the Soviet-supplied rockets for quick use, primarily against cities or large military complexes like Chu Lai. Their effectiveness was correspondingly reduced; most launches resulted in little substantive damage and few casualties. The rockets had degenerated into mere weapons of terror intended to strike at the morale of American troops by causing fear and uncertainty.

With dawn rapidly approaching, the PAVN soldiers relentlessly continued their work. All the soldiers were fully aware that the entire success of their mission was predicated upon surprise. As soon as the first rocket impacted within the Chu Lai compound, the Americans would scramble for cover and the base's alert sirens would shriek out a belated warning. The Chu Lai radar complex, strategically located on high ground near Division artillery, would quickly pinpoint the launch site and direct a deadly barrage of counter-fire which meant that speed was all the more imperative.

At 0550 hours, all the preparations for the launch had been finally completed with each of the rockets connected to a battery-operated detonator by a long, thin copper wire. The entire platoon silently moved away from the immediate launch area, seeking shelter wher-

PAUL STEPHANUS

Two ARVN soldiers examine a captured enemy 122mm rocket. The shrapnel-producing rocket was used primarily against large military complexes and big cities. Launch tubes increased the weapon's accuracy but were rarely used in the field.

ever it was available. A North Vietnamese officer gave an order and on command the first rocket suddenly sprang to life, shattering the pre-dawn silence and erupting into flame, momentarily illuminating the area with a fierce orange glow before propelling the missile into the morning sky. In rapid synchronization, the remaining missiles were launched.

At that same moment, 1st Lieutenant Sharon Lane, U.S. Army, had just completed the last of her rounds in Ward 4-B of the 312th Evacuation Hospital in Chu Lai. The petite, attractive Ohio-born nurse had been in-country for just six weeks and had only recently volunteered for the 12-hour night rotation on the Vietnamese ward. It was a noble endeavor since some of the other hospital personnel shunned this particular assignment being unable or unwilling to separate their bitterness against the Viet Cong and NVA who killed American GIs from their regard for the innocent, civilian Vietnamese.

For Lieutenant Lane, it had been a fairly routine night. The ward's 26 patients consisted mostly of women and children. They suffered from a variety of ailments ranging in severity from intestinal worms to life-threatening shrapnel wounds. Some required intensive monitoring while others had to be regularly charted and medicated. Those with serious injuries had to have their bandages periodically changed and their wounds dressed, a task greatly complicated by the ever-present language barrier. Now, finally, all of Lieutenant Lane's patients were asleep and the ward was quiet and peaceful. She knew that this was only a temporary respite. In just a few minutes, it would be time to awaken the Vietnamese patients for breakfast, and she would have to hurry to finish the ever-present paperwork before the next shift reported for duty at 0700 hours.

Still, Lieutenant Lane took advantage of the brief quiet to relax. She sat down on one of the ward's few empty beds and quietly chatted with a hospital corpsman, Cannon Sample. The 312th's on-duty officer, Captain Ed Welch, had earlier warned both of them that the Americal division headquarters had some intelligence warning of an impending attack on the Chu Lai compound by the North

Vietnamese. For much of the night, Lane, Sample, and most of the other medical personnel assigned to the 312th wore flak vests while tending to their patients. The vests were bulky, uncomfortable, and awkward, so gradually throughout the night, virtually everyone discarded them, taking solace in the fact that most rumors proved groundless.

As the light of first dawn appeared on the horizon, Sample abruptly left Lieutenant Lane's side and walked across the ward to a screen door in order to watch the sunrise. Dawn along the coast of the South China Sea was something to behold as the black of night was transformed into the light gray of daybreak, pink streaks of sunlight bathing the eastern horizon in a warm glow which was spectacularly reflected in the waves of the blue sea. As Sample left the ward expecting the quiet, contemplative serenity of sunrise, suddenly and without warning, the calm of the early morning was turned into chaos and pandemonium by a terrific explosion. One of the rockets launched by the NVA cadre landed directly on the connecting walkway between Wards 4A and 4B. Sample was blown through the doorway where he was standing by the force of the blast but, remarkably, was uninjured. Ward 4-B, however, had been instantly reduced to rubble with live electrical wires sparking dangerously near broken water pipes. Beds had been transformed into a tangled mess of steel and shredded mattresses, while the screams of the newly injured and re-wounded could still be heard over the piercing sound of the alert siren. Lieutenant Sharon Lane, 25 years old, lay silent and motionless in a rapidly growing pool of blood as her friends and co-workers climbed over wreckage and debris in a desperate effort to reach her. It was only a matter of seconds before the first medical personnel arrived and attempted to stop the bleeding. They all quietly knew, however, that there was little to be done for Sharon Lane had already bled to death after a piece of shrapnel had lacerated her carotid artery.

The PAVN troops quickly packed their gear. They could tell little from the distant sounds of explosions. Most likely, some of their rockets had missed the target and had fallen harmlessly into the South China Sea. The damage caused by the others would have to remain a mystery until Vietnamese informants on the Chu Lai base reported back with an assessment of the attack. For now, there was little time to think about such things for the U.S. artillery counter-fire would be swift and the day belonged to the Americans who would soon be coming.

2

America's Heartland

"Ike Told Reds Enter Laos from Viet Nam"
—Canton *Repository* (January 1961)

The state of Ohio derived its name from the Iroquois word meaning "good river." It had been neatly carved from the lush land that once comprised the old Northwest Territory, a region that the British ceded to the United States after the American Revolution. On March 1, 1803 during the presidency of Thomas Jefferson, Ohio was formally admitted to the union as the growing nation's 17th state. The people of the "Buckeye State" were deeply proud of their pioneer roots and, by the middle of the 19th century, they had developed a strong sense of patriotism fueled by their republican ideals and intense dislike of the system of slavery. In 1861, even before the sounds of the guns fired against Fort Sumter echoed into memory, 30,000 Ohio boys bravely answered President Lincoln's call for army volunteers, far exceeding the state's initial enlistment quota. For the next four long years as the American Civil War raged, Ohio's youth joined the Union army in ever-increasing numbers. They fought bravely in the fields of Manassas, died along the ridges of Gettysburg, suffered in the dense woods of the Wilderness, and held firm at Shiloh until the Confederacy was finally subdued. The human toll on the state was staggering: 35,475 Ohio citizens died during the bloody conflict.

With a return to peace, the Industrial Revolution caught fire and spawned an economic revival in the Midwest. Steel quickly became Ohio's chief industry, generating factories, jobs, and prosperity. Throughout the state, small frontier towns evolved into bustling cities as thousands immigrated to the state in a quest for economic opportunity. On the banks of the Cuyahoga River and Lake Erie, Cleveland became the center of the nation's booming oil industry and home to robber baron John D. Rockefeller's colossal corporation, Standard Oil Company of Ohio. At the same time, the nation's insatiable appetite for automobiles was being fed by both Akron and Dayton, while the city of Toledo became one of the nation's largest and most important railroad hubs.

Ohio's parochial pride was further enhanced by the substantial accomplishments of many of its notable citizens. Wilbur and Orville Wright, the developers of the airplane, lived and worked in Dayton; Thomas Alva Edison was born in Milan, Ohio, and invented the phonograph in 1887 while living in the state; and William Holmes McGuffey published in Cincinnati his famed series of readers that taught generations of young Americans to read. Other Ohioans were credited with developing and marketing such eclectic items as the padded bicycle seat, the traffic light, the vacuum cleaner, and Formica. Politically, the Buckeye state produced an impressive number of political leaders: eight Presidents, two vice-presidents, three Chief Justices, four Secretaries of State, and two Speakers of the House.

Just 60 miles to the south of Cleveland was the quaint, industrial city of Canton. Nestled in the gentle, rolling hills of Stark County, the city's population peaked in 1960 with 90,000 residents. Most were blue-collar workers employed by E.W. Bliss, Hercules Motors Corporation, Automatic Steel Products Incorporated, and other manufacturers. Despite its large number of smokestack industries, at the beginning of the 1960s, Canton offered many amenities to its inhabitants who enjoyed a high-quality, Midwestern life in the heartland of America. It was still possible to rent an apartment within the city limits for just $47 per month or purchase a modest, suburban, two-bedroom rambler for under $10,000. Canton's 26 parks included the impressive McKinley National Memorial, whose beautiful grounds contained an interesting array of fountains and ponds framing the gargantuan mausoleum of the nation's 25th president. Canton also counted 90 churches of varying denominations, 85 fraternal organizations, 4 high schools, 29 elementary schools, Malone College, and an extension of Kent State University in its area. Likewise, the city council was eagerly anticipating the onset of construction of the new Pro Football Hall of Fame, which had just been commissioned by the National Football League.

It was here in this small Ohio city that John and Kay Lane chose to settle and raise a family. The Lane's were married in Russell, Kentucky, on July 5, 1941. Within a few months, the newlyweds moved to south Canton where Mr. Lane secured employment as a truck driver with the Weaver Coal Company. When the business closed a few years later, he went to work with Dale Rogers and Sons as a bulldozer operator, excavating basements and doing landscaping.

All three of the Lane's children were born during World War II: first, Judy in 1942, followed by Sharon in 1943 and Gary in 1944. The Lane family initially lived in a small, rental apartment but soon purchased a building lot just a block away on 46th Street. Mr. Lane personally undertook the task of constructing a new home for his family, doing much of the labor himself with some help from Ash Davidson, a neighbor, close friend, and expert electrician.

By December 1951, the basement foundation of the Lane's new home was finally completed. It had been designed to be completely self-contained and was equipped with a kitchen, private bedrooms, and bathrooms, which enabled the entire family to move into the structure while Mr. Lane continued work on the yet-unfinished upper story. The entire house would not be completely framed and enclosed for another five years.

Life for the Lane children during the 1950s was fairly typical of the Cold War era. The children frequently played in the adjacent vacant fields, walked to the local elementary school, and grewup watching the "Mickey Mouse Club," "Ozzie and Harriet," and "American Bandstand" on television. Sharon had many interests, which included sewing and photography. She enjoyed bowling on weekends with friends and playing pool on the family's own basement pool table. As a teenager, Sharon listed in her memory book the names of her favorite rock-and-roll performers, including Fabian, Elvis, Dion, Paul Anka, and Ricky Nelson. Each night, she tuned in the local radio station and went to sleep to their music, enjoying the luxury of sleeping-in late whenever possible.

John Lane enjoyed an especially close relationship with his middle daughter, Sharon. The two would frequently go on day-long fishing expeditions to area lakes and ponds, enjoying the solitude and each other's company. They also spent many quiet hours on Sunday together in worship at south Canton's Methodist church.

Sharon completed her early education at North Industrial School and then enrolled at the nearby Canton South High School in September of 1957. Located on the corner of Cleveland Avenue and Faircrest Street, the high school was just a mile from the Lane's 46th Street residence. Because it was separated by busy Route 8, then Canton's main thoroughfare, however, the school board mandated that Sharon and other students living on the west side of the road should ride the schoolbus rather than negotiate the risky passage across a major highway.

Canton South High School was a majestic, brick structure, which had first opened its doors to students some 20 years earlier in 1937. Its spotless grounds were surrounded by acres of well-manicured playing fields; the classrooms were filled with books, test tubes, and maps, strongly suggesting that this school took both its academics and sports seriously. Directly opposite the high school was Jack's Quik Shake, a restaurant that catered to South's students by offering the traditional high school fare of hamburgers, french fries, and sodas in the era before fast-food restaurants. Dominating the other corner of the intersection was the imposing presence of the Kreighbaum Funeral Home.

KAY LANE

The Lane children—Gary, Judy, and Sharon—circa 1948. The family lived in South Canton where Mr. Lane worked as a heavy equipment operator excavating basements and doing landscape work.

PHILIP BIGLER

A contemporary photo of Canton South High School. The façade of the building remains virtually unchanged since the time when Sharon attended classes there from 1957 through 1961. Located only one mile from the Lane's residence on 46th Street, the school was a center of Sharon's social activities.

Sharon began her senior year at Canton South in the fall of 1960. It was a magical and exciting time to be a teenager in America. The nation was enjoying a relatively prosperous economy and was still brimming with pride, self-confidence, and optimism. Indeed, that very year, the United States had successfully placed in orbit *Echo I*, the world's first communications satellite; Harper Lee published the soon-to-be classic novel, *To Kill a Mockingbird*; the great Floyd Patterson successfully regained his heavyweight boxing championship; and the country was experiencing the rock-and-roll revolution in music. Chubby Checker's "The Twist" inspired an entirely new teen dance craze, while the peculiar song, "Itsy Bitsy Teenie Weenie Yellow Polka Dot Bikini," dominated the 1960 hit charts, much to the dismay of parents.

The biggest story of 1960 and the topic of many classroom discussions in Sharon's senior government class was the hotly contested presidential race between Vice-President Richard Nixon and Senator John F. Kennedy. A series of nationally televised debates had been carefully watched by an estimated audience of 70 million, and both candidates crisscrossed the nation in a desperate quest for votes. With its generous allotment of 25 electoral votes, Ohio was seen as a critical state for both candidates. Even though the state traditionally voted Republican, the presence of large numbers of blue-collar union workers concentrated in Ohio's urban areas gave the Democrats a realistic opportunity to carry the state on November 8. It was this hope that brought the young, dynamic Jack Kennedy to Canton on September 27.

Over 10,000 enthusiastic Kennedy supporters crammed into the city's Memorial Auditorium, an arena built to accommodate only half that number. Kennedy used the forum to talk about the need to stimulate the nation's economy and create new jobs, a message carefully crafted to appeal to the audience of predominately union workers. Despite Kennedy dramatic blitz through Ohio, Nixon still prevailed, carrying the state by a healthy margin in a losing national effort.

There was portentous news that autumn as well. Peaceful sit-in strikes were routinely being held in Greensboro, North Carolina, by African-American students protesting the nation's racial policies and demanding immediate progress on civil rights. Soviet Premier Nikita Khrushchev was making ominous pronouncements in Moscow following the celebrated show trial of American U-2 spy pilot, Francis Gary Powers. Fidel Castro, the young revolutionary who had seized power in Cuba, seemed to be moving incessantly toward establishing a communist dictatorship just 90 miles off the coast of Florida; he denounced the United States in a marathon 4½-hour tirade at the United Nations. Of lesser note was the news of a growing insurgency in distant South Vietnam against the corrupt administration of President Ngo Dinh Diem. Viet Cong guerrillas were becoming increasingly bold in their efforts to "liberate" the south and had just formed the National Liberation Front (NLF), prompting the Eisenhower administration to commit even more military advisers to the region.

For 17-year-old Sharon, these international developments were subordinate to the more immediate pressures of her final year of high school. She had a rigorous academic schedule which, along with her government class, included courses in world history, psychology, sociology, physics, and English. Sharon had earned a reputation as a solid, conscientious student who maintained a steady *B*-average. She faltered only in her science course where she struggled for a *C* but was able to counter-balance that grade with an *A* in Rose Marie Fulmer's psychology class.

Sharon's social life revolved almost entirely around high school events since she had yet to obtain her driver's license. She and her girlfriends always cheered enthusiastically at every scheduled Friday afternoon pep rally and went to virtually all of their beloved Wildcats' football games. The school was notorious for its poor teams, however, and had lost every contest the previous season. In 1960, Coach Don Nehlen managed to compile a respectable 4-4-1 season. The highlight of the year was the team's decisive victory over rival Louisville High School, a game in which Ed Peterson starred with an impressive four-touchdown performance.

On weekends, Sharon often hosted sleepovers for her girl friends. They would talk late into the night about boys, listen to music, and gossip about the year's biggest scandal—a beer party involving a group of rowdy seniors. They would also go bowling or to the Dairy Isle for ice cream. At the movies, they saw such hits as *The World of Suzie Wong*, *Butterfield 8*, and *The Wackiest Ship in the Army*. On more daring occasions, at the East 30 Drive-in, the teenagers saw Alfred Hitchcock's thriller, *Psycho*. It was a carefree time of good fun and innocence.

During that last school year, the months seemed to pass more quickly than most, punctuated by Red Ash's basketball team winning the league championship with a 10-point victory over Sandy Valley, 63-53, front page news in the local Canton *Repository*. The school's drama department staged the perennial hit, *Oklahoma*, and the prom, the social event of the year, was held in May at the romantic Moonlight Ballroom at Meyers Lake Park with the theme, "Stairway to the Stars." Before Sharon and her classmates knew it, the 1961 version of the *Moderian* yearbook had arrived. The graduating seniors passed their copies around, having them autographed as a memento of their last year of high school. Sharon's own copy was generously signed with most people noting that she was a "sweet and caring person."

On May 31, the South Canton High School Class of 1961 gathered for its final time in the school's gymnasium for graduation ceremonies. The students were resplendent in their cap and gowns, optimistic about the future but a bit nervous about leaving behind the comfortable sanctuary of high school. The students proudly marched to their seats as the band played the traditional "Pomp and Circumstance." As with all such rites of passage, the scheduled program dragged on forever aggravated by the fact that the featured speaker, Frank Shaheen, had chosen the bizarre topic, "Conservatism and Liberalism," as the subject of his commencement address. Finally, the superintendent of schools, Ray Graham, handed the graduates individually a diploma certifying their completion of high school. The most dramatic and moving moment of the ceremonies came near the end when Sandy Young's name was announced. Parents, teachers, and students cheered wildly, many with tears in their eyes, as Sandy slowly walked across the stage, winning a

Sharon's senior yearbook photo. She graduated from Canton South on May 31st, 1961 and decided to enroll that fall in the three year nursing program offered at nearby Aultman Hospital.

personal triumph over the cancer that she had been battling for years. With the closing of the ceremonies, the Canton South students hugged each other good-bye before adjourning to meet with their families and friends for private celebrations. Sharon Lane, like most of her fellow graduates, now had to ponder what lay ahead; it was time to decide what to do with the rest of her life.

The onset of John F. Kennedy's "New Frontier" had little immediate effect on American society. Although Kennedy's administration seemed to exude youth and vigor, there were few substantive opportunities in the United States for young women after they graduated from high school in the 1960s. It was still common for many girls to marry almost immediately, begin families, and assume the traditional role of housewives. For those who remained single, hundreds of business schools attempted to lure them with a curricula of shorthand and typing and with shallow promises of a "satisfying life" as a business secretary. Many young women opted to enroll at four-year colleges and universities but, once on campus, found themselves quickly channeled away from male-dominated disciplines such as engineering, architecture, and science. Instead, they were encouraged to major in home economics or elementary education. The only other real, viable option was nursing school.

Sharon considered all these options before finally enrolling at the nurses' training program offered by Canton's Aultman Hospital, a facility located just seven miles from her home. The rigorous three-year program was modeled on the concept developed at the turn of the century by the famed Florence Nightingale which blended a palatable amount of medical theory with direct patient contact. Using this apprentice-type system, Aultman's School of Nursing had earned a solid reputation for turning out high-quality, competent nurses.

After a brief summer vacation, Sharon joined 58 other anxious girls in the new, entering freshmen class at Morrow House, the school's combined dorm and classroom facility. Located on 6th

Street immediately adjacent to the massive hospital complex, the rules of the residence were strict with curfews imposed, dress codes enforced, and demerits issued. Sharon and her new roommate, Barb, were assigned a spartan room furnished only with twin beds, two desks, a sink, and a single dresser. They immediately attempted to make it more comfortable and hospitable by hanging new drapes and filling the room with a wide variety of stuffed animals. Their decorations also included an aquarium equipped with two goldfish and several guppies. Despite their best efforts, the room also came with an ample supply of silverfish and even an occasional roach.

The first year of Aultman's nursing program consisted primarily of course and class work. The limited patient contact was confined to observing other nurses in the hospital performing routine procedures and to learn such mundane tasks as giving baths to patients and making their beds. Most of the academic lectures that the student-nurses were required to attend were held in the Morrow House classrooms. Some courses were taught at the nearby Malone College campus. In those cases, the nurses boarded hospital buses to attend these classes.

Sharon and her classmates were first expected to learn all of the body's major organs and their functions along with the basics of the circulatory and respiratory systems. Anatomy proved to be one of the most challenging courses required during the first year, albeit one of the most essential. Sharon's professor, much to her amusement, would occasionally wander off on a tangent during lectures about the research he was currently conducting, grafting amputated reptile limbs onto salamanders in an effort to regenerate the extremities. Most of the instruction was far more relevant and challenging. As part of the course work, Sharon and her lab partner dissected a frog in class and used pins with small flags to identify all of its anatomical parts. In an effort to prepare for the scheduled exam, Sharon smuggled out another dead frog and repeated the dissection in her room, relabeling all of the organs in order to study more completely. To preserve the mutilated frog, she stored it on her dorm room's window sill, relying on Ohio's autumn weather to keep it cool. She later confided in a letter to her good friend, Doris

Plastow, "These warm nights are kind of hard on (the frog) though."

Besides her academic classes, Sharon was expected to attend other routine lectures scheduled by the school on a wide variety of topics. One of the more eclectic was entitled, "Good Grooming," where the lecturer emphasized the need for young girls to dress modestly and in good taste in order to have a successful career. This message was all the more bizarre since the girls' nursing uniforms allowed little room for modification or creativity. Sharon recorded some of the other advice given to the students, ". . . (young women should) always wear heels—flats are for younger girls; never wear eye makeup to work; never, *never* wear red nail polish to work; don't wear your skirts too long or too short; wear a neat and natural-looking hairstyle. She says if you follow these suggestions you will be able to obtain and retain a good secretarial job, but who wants an office job?!"

There was a lot of good-natured teasing of the new freshman students by the upper classmen at the Morrow House. The younger girls were initiated into the nursing profession by being required to dress up in outlandish outfits and wear demerit sheets on their clothes. They were expected to bow when they passed the older girls and endure other good-natured, harmless hazing.

Still, Sharon's first year at Aultman consisted of a lot of studying and hard work. She soon developed serious doubts about her choice of careers and was ambivalent about continuing. She confided in a letter, "This place gives me mixed emotions. Half of the time I like it and am glad I got in here and all, and the other half of the time I wish I was at home going to good old South . . . South was really a pretty good place after all, huh?" In fact, Sharon continued to spend most of her off-duty weekends at home with her family and still regularly attended most of the Canton South High School's sporting events, even keeping a scrapbook of the on-field heroics. After completing a semester of course work in the Aultman Nursing Program, Sharon decided to take a six-month leave of absence to reassess her situation.

——— ✯ ———

Sharon's sabbatical from nursing lasted only a few months. When she decided to return to the Morrow House at the beginning of the next school year, she was ahead of most of the other girls both in age and course work. As a result, she was paired with a new roommate, Penny Lopez, from Massillon, Ohio, who was in a similar situation.

The second and third years of the Aultman program proved even more intensive than the first. Sharon was assigned to work on various floors of the hospital during three-month rotations, concentrating on a specific discipline. She was taught how to draw blood, check blood pressure, and administer proper medication. At the same time, she studied the basics of dietary service and was expected to continue with her scheduled academic classes. One three-month training period was required at the Ohio State Mental Hospital in Massillon, the only time that Sharon was away from the actual Aultman Hospital complex. The work was hard, the hours were long, and there were few holidays.

Sharon's daily routine consisted of working on the ward she was assigned and attending classes. In the late afternoon, she would usually go back to her dorm room to take a short nap before eating dinner in the Morrow House cafeteria. Most of her evenings were devoted to studying or working a late shift at the hospital. Occasionally, Sharon and Penny would go out for ice cream or even cook a homemade pizza in the dorm's basement kitchen. The girls always tried to make time to catch their favorite television program, "Route 66," on the Morrow House's color TV. It was one of the few luxuries afforded to the student nurses.

Since Sharon had reentered the Aultman program, she completed her course requirements before the other girls in her new class. She even successfully passed her state nursing board exams before graduating in April 1965. Like many other girls, she was offered full-time employment with the hospital as a registered nurse. This opportunity posed an immediate problem for Sharon since she did not have her driver's license and would be expected to commute to

KAY LANE

Sharon's graduation photo from the Aultman School of Nursing. After finishing the rigorous program and passing her nursing boards, she was offered employment with the hospital in its obstetrics ward. She purchased a black, used Corvair to commute to work from her home in South Canton.

work from her home in south Canton. She immediately purchased a black Corvair, Chevrolet's innovative rear-engine car with sporty bucket seats that was being marketed for young professionals. Shortly thereafter, Sharon finally succeeded in obtaining her driver's license. Everything now seemed to be in place: Sharon had a degree, a car, and a new career in medicine. It was spring, 1965.

3

In the Army

"The [Tet] attacks enhanced the mystique of the Viet Cong as a stealthy, dedicated foe, unmindful of death."
—*Time* Magazine (February 16, 1968)

In many ways, the dramatic scene resembled the historic landing of General Douglas MacArthur at Leyte Gulf some 21 years earlier. Yet, no pitched battle had preceded the two battalions of U.S. Marines as they waded through the surf clutching their M-14 rifles onto the sandy beaches of Da Nang harbor. Instead, they were met by a peaceful contingent of local dignitaries, who welcomed them to Vietnam, and by several beautiful Vietnamese girls in silk gowns. It was an incongruous sight: heavily armed U.S. Marines surrounded by scores of civilians, newsmen, and photographers with the enemy nowhere to be seen.

The landing of the 3,500 American combat soldiers in Vietnam on March 9, 1965, was a major escalation of the conflict. President Lyndon Johnson had reluctantly ordered the action only after he had received reliable intelligence advising him that the war would be lost without direct American intervention. The current ambassador, General Maxwell Taylor, had relayed several ominous reports to Washington confirming these fears and warning of increased Communist infiltration of the south along the Ho Chi Minh trail. It was predicted that the American-backed ARVN troops could do little to interdict the flow. Even with the addition of American air support, little could be done to disrupt the growing strength of the enemy.

Emboldened by the Gulf of Tonkin Resolution passed by Congress that effectively ceded war-making powers to the President the previous year, Johnson attempted to pursue a policy of gradual escalation of American involvement in the war in Southeast Asia. After five American advisers were killed by the Viet Cong at Bien Hoa and eight more were killed at Pleiku in February 1965, the President first ordered U.S. planes to launch retaliatory raids against military and strategic targets in North Vietnam. On March 2, Operation *Rolling Thunder* commenced a fierce and continuous bombing above the 17th parallel. It was destined to last for the next three years but produced only modest results. The landing of the U.S. Marines at Da Nang just a few days later was an integral part of the administration's new, get-tough strategy in Vietnam, but it simultaneously gave impetus to the burgeoning antiwar movement in the United States.

By April 1965, military draft quotas had been considerably increased and hundreds of new troops were being shipped daily to Vietnam. The President decided to give a major foreign policy address at Johns Hopkins University in Maryland to explain the war in Vietnam to the American people in terms of the greater context of the ongoing Cold War between the United States and the Communist world. "Why must this Nation hazard its ease, and interest, and its power for the sake of a people far away?" Johnson asked. "North Vietnam has attacked the independent nation of South Vietnam. Its object is total conquest . . . Over this war—and all Asia— is another reality: the deepening shadow of Communist China. The rulers in Hanoi are urged on by Peking. This is a regime which has destroyed freedom in Tibet, which has attacked India, and has been condemned by the United Nations for aggression in Korea. It is a nation which is helping the forces of violence in almost every continent. The contest in Vietnam is part of a wider pattern of aggressive purposes."

Johnson's passionate appeal did little to quell the voices of dissent. Just ten days later, 15,000 antiwar demonstrators gathered in Washington, D.C. to oppose the administration's Asian policies. Soon, Ivy League colleges, Berkeley, and other elite universities were staging "teach-ins" against the war while American troop strength was approaching 75,000.

The new domestic unrest did not alter the overall mission of the military in Vietnam. With the deep water port of Da Nang fully secured, the Pentagon began to make initial preparations for the construction of a series of major airbases to support infantry operations throughout the country. In the I-Corps region, the military area closest to the 17th parallel, it was decided that such a base had to be located along the coast and completely supportable by sea. Although Highway One, the French-built 1,056-mile road from Saigon to Hanoi, cut through the region, the road was extremely primitive by American standards and the military deemed it unsuitable to handle the vast volume of traffic required to support a major military base. Furthermore, the road was constantly vulnerable to disruption by snipers, enemy mines, and Viet Cong attack.

Dung Quat Bay, a shallow-draught harbor some 60 miles south of Da Nang, seemed a promising location for a U.S. Marine air support base. The Third Marine Division was sent to the area to secure it from the enemy and to relocate some 400 peasant villagers who lived in the immediate area. As military sweeping operations continued in the vicinity, Navy Mobile Construction Battalion Ten landed at the site with bulldozers and other heavy construction equipment. The Seabees were under orders to construct a jet-capable, 8,000-foot runway within three weeks and to build 12 miles of support roads and two helicopter pads.

On May 7, 1965, Navy engineers staked out the perimeter of the planned Chu Lai airfield in the soft, sandy soil. Work commenced almost immediately, hampered by the region's oppressive heat and humidity. With daytime temperatures regularly soaring to over 100 degrees, the men could work for just 30 minutes before needing to be relieved. As a result, it required two full shifts of Seabees to complete the normal 12-hour workday. Further complicating the construction was the constant problem of wind-blown sand that clogged the carburetors of heavy equipment and trucks. It was estimated that fully 50 percent of all equipment was inoperable at any given time.

Still, the Seabees did a remarkable job of leveling the terrain and laying a prefabricated, interlocking, aluminum-mat runway. Despite more problems with shifting sands and the resultant potholes, 4,000 feet of the runway were completed by June 1. That very morning, Colonel John Noble, United States Marine Corps, landed the first A-4 *Skyhawk*, which was joined later by a squadron of seven planes. By that afternoon, U.S. Marine pilots were flying support operations for the infantry. The full 8,000 feet of runway became completely operational on July 3, and Chu Lai was well on its way to becoming one of the largest and most critical American bases in Vietnam.

In that same spring of 1965, Sharon Lane was beginning her new nursing career at Aultman Hospital. As a board-certified nurse, her primary responsibility was in obstetrics where she was assigned to work with new mothers, although she would have an assignment in the nursery. For Sharon, the days at the hospital soon proved long, tedious, and routine, consisting primarily of tending to the seemingly endless needs and whims of new mothers rather than in applying her medical skills. She did her assigned duties well, though, and was well-liked by her patients and their families. Her coworkers remembered Sharon fondly as a talented and gifted nurse, competent and professional. But still, Sharon saw her life as unfulfilling. Most of her closest high school friends had either moved away or were now busy with new family commitments or their own careers. Sharon felt her professional life had degenerated into the daily grind of commuting to the hospital, working on the ward, and coming home to sleep—an endless and unsatisfying cycle for a 22-year old woman.

After just two years with Aultman hospital, Sharon quit her job to enroll at Canton Business College and began training as a secre-

A topographical map of the Chu Lai area. The Marine airbase was built along the coast of the South China Sea and soon, the base developed into one of the largest and most important American facilities in Vietnam.

tary. This, too, quickly proved to be a disillusionment, and after nine months, Sharon firmly concluded that she was not destined to spend the rest of her life behind a typewriter.

In early 1968, after spending an evening out with a friend, Sharon returned home and announced to her shocked parents that she planned on enlisting in the U.S. Army. Although she had never expressed even the remotest interest in a military career, the promise of working as an Army nurse had a great deal of appeal, offering potential travel to exotic places and assignment to posts in different parts of the United States. Military recruiters were, in fact, desperate to fill large numbers of nursing vacancies because of severe shortages caused by the ongoing Vietnam War. Also there were many stateside positions available at such locations as Walter Reed Hospital in suburban Washington, D.C. and Fitzsimons Hospital in Denver, Colorado. Certainly no newly enlisted Army nurse was predestined for stationing in Southeast Asia.

Sharon had intended to enlist with her friend and complete their basic training together, but this idea quickly disintegrated when the other girl's parents steadfastly refused to allow her to join the U.S. Army. Sharon, though, had firmly made up her mind and went down alone to the Army recruiter's office in Canton and signed the appropriate papers on April 18. Although her routine physical showed that she had a slight heart murmur, probably caused by a bout with rheumatic fever as a child, she was deemed fit for active duty and was instructed to report to Fort Sam Houston in San Antonio, Texas, in early May.

In Vietnam, 1968, the "Year of the Monkey," had begun ominously with the Tet Offensive, an all-out assault on American positions throughout the South Vietnam. The Republic's major cities were attacked by the Communist forces as were hundreds of firebases, military installations, and even hospital compounds. Despite initial military setbacks, the campaign resulted in a tactical defeat for the enemy with NVA and Viet Cong losses estimated at over 40,000

KAY LANE

Sharon at the Cleveland Zoo in April, 1968, shortly after her enlistment in the US Army. She was ordered to report to Fort Sam Houston in Texas for training.

killed of the approximately 84,000 engaged. Politically, however, the bold Communist strike had been brutally effective. President Johnson's popularity plummeted to an all-time low of just 36 percent and once again, American college campuses spasmodically erupted in antiwar demonstrations. Faced with potential humiliation at the polls, Johnson announced on March 31 that he would no longer seek reelection.

Finally freed from the political concerns that governed his decisions on waging the war, the President began to reassess the military situation in Vietnam. General William Westmoreland, the overall commander of U.S. forces, had requested after Tet that the President commit an additional 200,000 troops to the conflict, something that Johnson believed untenable. Instead, he finally ordered the mobilization of 20,034 reservists, the first such call-up since 1961.

The President's action had been authorized in 1967 by the Russell Amendment, a little known Congressional rider that had been quietly attached to a major fiscal appropriations bill. The newly enacted law gave the President the sole authority to activate the military reserves at any time through June 30, 1968, for a period not to exceed 24 months. Such extraordinary action had historically been reserved only for times of clear national peril such as President Kennedy's call-up during the critical Berlin crisis of 1961 and President Truman's activation of the reserves during the Korean Conflict. Until 1968, President Johnson had consistently and steadfastly opposed using the reserves in Vietnam because he feared that a major military mobilization would focus public attention on an increasingly unpopular war while detracting from his far-reaching domestic agenda. Furthermore, the President feared that it would lead the American people to demand an immediate victory or complete withdrawal from Southeast Asia, something that ran contrary to the administration's policy of gradual escalation.

For the early years of the Vietnam War, it was ironic that the war was being waged by young draftees, whereas military reserve units became a haven for thousands of draft-evaders, content to serve out their six-year commitment on weekends within the safe confines of the United States. By its own estimation, the Pentagon maintained that fully 71 percent of all reservists had joined their units to avoid service in Vietnam. The National Guard was similarly safe from deployment overseas, primarily because it was often needed to quell the widening domestic unrest in American cities and campuses.

After Tet, however, military necessity and logic demanded the call-up of the reserves. The units were staffed by older, more mature soldiers, and they possessed a strong sense of unit cohesion. The reservists were well-trained and could be rapidly deployed within just a few weeks of activation. Thus, President Johnson issued the fateful order on April 8, 1968 calling some 20,000 reservists to active duty. In an effort to lessen the impact of the move, the call-up involved 76 units spread over 34 states.

The announcement had little immediate impact and the reaction from the American public was surprisingly subdued. Other events, far more momentous, had temporarily commanded the national attention. Just four days earlier, the great civil rights activist, Dr. Martin Luther King, had been assassinated in Memphis, Tennessee. Racial riots erupted in the nation's capital and in dozens of other American cities; students at Columbia University in New York seized the college's administrative offices in protest of the war; and a new presidential poll showed that in a two-man race, Senator Robert F. Kennedy would defeat Richard M. Nixon in the forthcoming election. While college students at Duke University in North Carolina were actively engaged in a sit-in strike, a high school principal made headlines by convening a five-member teacher committee to enforce a proscription against teenage girls wearing their dresses hemmed more than two inches above the knee.

In Winston-Salem, a small, provincial, southern town known primarily for its booming cigarette industry and as the home of Wake Forest University, Johnson's activation of the Army reserves held severe consequences. Home to the 312th Evacuation Hospital, a medical unit first created in 1924 which served during both World War II and the Korean Conflict, it was one of the first targeted for duty in Vietnam. Incredibly, the word of the unit's impending deployment was first announced publicly by North Carolina's elected representatives and widely reported over the radio before ever being channeled through official military sources. Cannon Sample, one of the 312th reservists, had been married for just six months and was working in his father's dental clinic when he heard the news that his unit had been activated by the Johnson call-up. The 300 soldiers, physicians, nurses, other officers, and enlisted personnel were instructed to report to the armory on Stadium Drive and were given just one month to make all of the necessary personal and professional arrangements before being shipped out to Vietnam.

Sharon arrived at Fort Sam Houston as ordered in early May, 1968. She had driven the entire distance alone, her black Corvair packed full with all of her essential belongings. The trip had been uneventful, except for one incident when her car broke down outside Columbus, just a couple of hours away from home.

Fort Sam Houston was a spawling military base located in San Antonio, Texas. It functioned as the Army's primary training facility for inducting medical personnel. The basic training program was intended to help doctors and nurses make the transition to the Army, to learn basic soldiering and survival skills, and to learn the rudiments of treating war wounds. Initially, the basic mechanics of Army life seemed daunting. Sharon wrote, ". . . we have to learn to salute and learn whom to salute and all that. This major told us if you don't know who to salute to 'salute anything that moves until you know better'."

Sharon was commissioned a 2nd Lieutenant on May 2 and spent the next few days filling out countless forms to feed the Army's legendary bureaucracy. Her service number, N-2-337-550, became her primary identity embedded forever in her memory.

The new soldiers were first taken down to the supply depot where they were each handed an empty, olive-green duffel bag. In assembly-line fashion, they received their allotment of fatigues, socks, boots, shirts, gloves, and hats. To the disappointment of Sharon and the other women, the only thing missing was a combat helmet.

An aerial view of the Fort Sam Houston medical training facilities circa 1968. The base was the Army's primary training facility for inducting medical personnel during the Vietnam War.

The nurses were likewise fitted for the Army's standard light-green cord uniform complete with the four-leaf clover insignia of the Fourth Army as well as for their hospital whites and dress blues. They were then photographed for their military identification cards.

Although officially assigned to the Brooke Army Medical Center, Sharon lived in Reid Hall, an undistinguished four-story facility conveniently located immediately adjacent to the post's hospital. There were only 36 people in this new class of recruits, including 5 male nurses, and as a result, only the lower two floors of the barracks were in use for housing with the upper stories left vacant. The raging war in Vietnam and the ever-increasing militancy of the antiwar movement had exacted a toll on the U.S. Army and made it exceedingly difficult to enlist needed medical personnel. Yet, just a few years earlier, Fort Sam Houston had been overflowing with volunteers. Typical classes then had up to 300 new recruits, numbers which strained the Army's housing facilities to the limit and often necessitated the military to contract rooms off-post in private motels. Those days, however, were now in the distant past.

The Vietnam War, invisible to much of American society except on television, was very much in evidence at Fort Sam Houston in 1968. All of the new U.S. Army nurses were expected to donate blood for those wounded in the war since the base hospital was serving as a major treatment and convalescent center for burn patients and other American casualties. Sharon confided, "From now on I will feel much more sympathetic when I go around sticking someone with a #18 needle."

For the young, inexperienced officer-nurses, it was a sobering experience to actually see the human residue of modern war. Sharon wrote, "Outside the hospital in the yard, there are always guys sitting who are back from [Vietnam] and they have leg amputations, arm amputations, etc. They really look pathetic. If they send me over there right away, I will probably be scared green—not of the fighting but at what I'm supposed to do for them. There is a captain living on our floor who just got back from her year in Vietnam and she was telling us about how you work 12 hours a day and get 1 day off a week and such. She loved it and didn't want to leave. She is changing from the Fourth Army—what I am in—to the First Army division because they are on orders to Vietnam. I suppose when you know what to do & etc. it isn't so bad." In fact, many of the nurses in Sharon's class had enlisted with the specific intent of requesting duty in Vietnam after basic training.

Early in the basic training program, it seemed that all the nurses did was receive vaccinations, polish their brass, stand for inspection, and march around post in their obviously new fatigues and combat boots. In a letter to her parents, Sharon wrote, "Our marching was terrible, but it is improving by now. I still can't do an 'about face' right. I almost fall on my face every time."

Their first classes were confined to map reading, U.S. Army Nurse Corps history, battle tactics, and other military subjects because, as one officer succinctly put it, "Nurses you already are; Army officers is what we want to make of you." Soon they were detailed to work an occasional shift inside the hospital and began serious training in wartime medical procedures including triage. The nurses were even taught how to conduct emergency surgical operations, such as tracheotomies, cut-downs, and debridements. In order to practice these delicate procedures, anesthetized goats were brought into labs for each nurse to practice on. Some had been shot to simulate typical wartime injuries. "Today we did the tracheotomies (surgical airways) on the goats," Sharon wrote, "and did gun shot wound debridements. These goats were alive but under anesthesia and they had shot them in the hind legs with an M-14 rifle, like is used in Viet Nam. Then we each had to take a wound and play like surgeons and cut out all the dead tissue, blood clots, tie off bleeders and such. I enjoyed it and think everyone did. We won't have to do it in Viet Nam unless the doctors get swamped. It is a good thing because we don't know enough about debriding. I was cutting away on this muscle and cut a fairly large vessel by accident. Therefore, there was blood all over the place. Our poor goat had 6 traches (holes in the windpipe) done on him, and he was getting in rather bad shape by the time we finished. Apparently they are put to death and then cremated following the class. Thank heaven."

More routinely, the nurses practiced on each other drawing small amounts of blood, a procedure which would be needed to perform lab tests on patients. Although a relatively simple operation compared to surgery, their early efforts often produced enormous bruises and other complications. In a letter home, Sharon wrote, "Monday in class we took blood samples from each other to learn how to draw blood for lab tests. Janice gave Barb a 'huge-type' bruise where she took hers. I took blood from this girl . . . from North or South Dakota. I did rather poorly, but got enough blood to pass. She did real good on getting mine but afterwards I got an inflamed vein and got a red streak up my hand to the wrist. I thought I'd go to the doctor when it got to my elbow but it never did—[it] just went away."

Besides their medical training, the nurses and other medical personnel were taught basic skills on how to survive in a combat zone. Since hospital compounds were intentionally targeted by the North Vietnamese during the recent Tet Offensive, elementary instruction was provided on how to shoot a .45-caliber pistol. The students were also taken to the firing range where they watched demonstrations of the new M-16 rifle and other military weapons.

The field maneuvers conducted at nearby Camp Bullis, 20 miles northwest of San Antonio, were some of the most practical military training. Sharon and her classmates were bused there in early June to visit the site of a mock Vietnamese village, which had been carefully reconstructed on the post. Although somewhat peculiar in the Texas countryside, it nevertheless provided an accurate representation of the typical living conditions of the Vietnamese people frequently encountered by American military personnel. Furthermore, some doctors and nurses would volunteer to visit such areas while in-country during humanitarian Medical Civic Action Programs (MEDCAP). These operations were intended to bring 20th-century health care to the peasant populations who often suffered from a variety of diseases and ailments ranging from tuberculosis to typhus. Most of these illnesses responded well to modern medical treatment, and it was hoped that these efforts by the U.S. Army would help indirectly win the people's "hearts and minds" to the American cause.

The village at Camp Bullis appeared to be peaceful and harmless to the untrained eye. As the nurses disembarked from the safety of their buses, this exercise initially seemed to be an exotic and novel outing, a break from their traditional routine; but its intended purpose was far more deliberate. Carefully concealed in some of the village's many haystacks were guerrillas ready to simulate an ambush; pits full of deadly punji sticks were camouflaged to illustrate cleverly concealed booby traps; and trip wires were strategically positioned to show the ever-present danger of mines. Sharon wrote, "This past week we spent on field maneuvers out at Camp Bullis. Monday we watched army weapons being fired—submachine guns, M-16 rifles, and such. Then we went into a simulated Vietnamese village rigged with booby traps by the Viet Cong. Of course old big-footed-elephant me stepped on a wire that set off a mine in this haystack. There was a loud explosion and smoke went up. Of course if it had been real, I would be [up] or [down]." In fact, many of the war wounds American soldiers received while in Vietnam were the result of just such booby traps and mines encountered in so-called pacified villages. The important and indelible lesson learned that day was that there were no safe areas in Vietnam and that there were many ways to die.

During their week-long training at Camp Bullis, the nurses were given instruction on how to set up and run a mobile field hospital. This consisted initially of erecting a large tent to house patients, a task that proved to be both difficult and awkward. Sharon wrote, "We had to lower and then reraise a hospital tent. The guys made it look so easy, but man is it hard to do! I positively could not set up my pole and this soldier had to come over and help me. Then we set up cots and took care of fake casualty patients. It was fun. However, Viet Nam won't be fun, I know."

As a final military exercise after having received detailed instruction on using a compass and map-reading, all the recruits were expected to pass a survival test. The entire class was broken down into smaller groups and provided with a map, two compasses, and

A mock Vietnamese village at Camp Bullis, Texas. Sharon and her classmates were bused to the site in June, 1968 for further military training.

Concealed in a haystack, an American soldier simulates a VC ambush. The mock village also contained punji sticks, booby-traps, and trip wires. Sharon tripped over one such device and detonated a dummy mine.

a canteen. They were then driven a short way out into the desert and abandoned. Using their meager equipment, each group was expected to navigate independently its way back to a predetermined location. There was little real danger involved, but the Army still kept a careful watch for any potential trouble and stood ready to rescue any group in distress. "They divided us up into 14 groups of four people per group and we had a map course to follow," Sharon wrote to her friend, Doris Plastow. "My group got along real well." It included her best friends, Janice and Barbara. They began the exercise at 0830 hours; it took them, despite their best efforts, well over three hours to reach their objective. Sharon continued, "We got a 99% on the course but were next to last to arrive at the required destination. We walked about three miles in fatigues, combat boots, helmets, and packs, but it was a lot of fun. These two helicopters flew over the area all the time to pick up any group that got lost or hurt. One girl got a big tarantula on her back. Where it came from I don't know. However, another brave soul got it off for her before it bit her. They warned us considerably to watch out for snakes but we never saw one (our group) and we really watched out for them, too."

The adjustment to U.S. Army life had gone surprisingly well for Sharon. It was made easier by the fact that she had made two very close friends while at Fort Sam Houston, Janice and Barbara. Janice was a nurse from North Carolina and had, like Sharon, driven her own car across country to Texas. She was planning on going to Vietnam immediately after basic training to join her brother who was already stationed there. Barbara was from Virginia and had been promised an assignment near her home so that she could be close to her fiancé.

The three women became virtually inseparable during their off-duty hours while at Fort Sam. They often took sightseeing excursions into San Antonio where they visited such sites as the Brackenridge Zoo and the city's newest attraction, Hemisfair. Likewise, they would frequently drive off post to eat at local restaurants, seeking a brief respite from the traditional bland, dining-hall fare. During one excursion, Sharon had her first experience with Texas's infamous Lone Star beer. She described it as ". . . tast[ing] exactly like the zoo smelled. I nearly threw up. Its the worst beer I've had yet."

The combination of good friends and intense military training made the time pass quickly for Sharon. She was ambivalent about finishing her six-week basic training course because she knew it would mean leaving San Antonio and losing the camaraderie she enjoyed with Janice and Barbara. Still, the Texas heat and humidity of early June had descended on the barracks with a vengeance and left everyone exhausted and short-tempered. It was time to go.

On Friday, June 14, the base held its formal graduation for this small class of 36. The ceremonies were succinct but appropriate with the Brooke Army Band providing the music. The most significant moment of the ceremonies came with the announcement and recognition of the top students. Carol Birdsell of Minnesota received top honors and both Janice and Barbara ranked in the top five. It was a joyous occasion, and there was a great deal of excitement as orders were issued to the new U.S. Army officers. Twelve of the nurses were destined for Vietnam service while six were detailed to hospitals in Japan. One was being sent to Hawaii, another to Okinawa, and 16 were being stationed at various posts within the continental United States. Sharon was in the last category having been assigned, as requested, to Fitzsimons Hospital in Denver, Colorado.

All that was left to do was to say good-bye. Most did not linger but departed quickly amid hugs and tears. Janice took Barbara to the airport before setting off in her Chevy Camaro to San Francisco. She hoped to make the trip on just $100 and planned on following a deep southern route in an effort to avoid the Arizona desert, which she desperately did not want to cross in a car without air conditioning.

Sharon was left alone to finish packing at the post's BOQ. She left later that day dressed casually in civilian clothes and began her trip north to Colorado and her first duty station as a 2nd Lieutenant, U.S. Army.

4

Orders—Vietnam

"The enemy has been defeated in battle after battle."
—Lyndon B. Johnson, State of the Union
(January 17, 1968)

The American base at Chu Lai had evolved into a mammoth military complex by 1968, encompassing over 36 square miles of land. Yet, it had only been three years since the U.S. Marines had first secured an outpost in the region and established a "rocket belt" around the newly constructed airfield. Kept free of enemy troops, the immediate vicinity around the base was firmly in American control. For a while, Chu Lai operated effectively and efficiently, out of range of some of the Viet Cong's most favored weapons, the Chicom (Chinese Communist) 107-mm rocket and 60-mm mortar. In early 1967, military intelligence revealed that, for the first time, the Communists had begun to deploy a dangerous new weapon, the Soviet-built 122-mm rocket, south of the 17th parallel. Designed as a high-trajectory missile with an effective range of up to six miles, these deadly shrapnel-producing projectiles could be fired with virtual impunity against high-density targets, such as military bases and large cities. As a result, they would continually pose a threat to the tranquillity of Chu Lai.

During that same year, the U.S. Army assumed the primary responsibility for the base and it became the headquarters of the famed Americal Division (23rd Infantry), the only named division during the war. The unit had been originally created by General Douglas MacArthur from American forces stationed on New Caledonia in the Pacific during the darkest hours of World War II and its impressive lineage included many of the most important campaigns waged against the Japanese in the Pacific from Guadalcanal to the Philippines. The airbase at Chu Lai, however, remained under U.S. Marine jurisdiction and was in perpetual use, launching daily sorties against enemy strongholds with A-4 *Skyhawks*, A-6 *Intruders*, and F-4 *Phantoms*. The U.S. Navy similarly maintained a large presence at Chu Lai, operating a shallow-water port to ensure the constant flow of supplies to the American forces deployed in the southern I-Corps region.

The buildup of Chu Lai and the surrounding areas directly corresponded with the rapid increase of American forces in Vietnam. From 1965 through 1968, the United States literally transformed the Vietnamese countryside by constructing hundreds of miles of roads and by building 6 deep water ports, 75 airfields, and countless numbers of firebases. At the same time, to handle the ever-increasing number of American casualties, the military established 24 hospitals throughout the south with a 5,283-bed capacity which were under the command of the 44th Medical Brigade headquartered in Long Binh, some 20 miles north of Saigon. In addition, two U.S. Navy hospital ships, *Repose* and *Sanctuary*, routinely rotated service in Vietnamese northern coastal waters.

Three types of American medical facilities were available in Vietnam. Each had a specific Table of Distribution (TOD), which detailed its allotment of doctors, nurses, and hospital beds. The smallest American medical compounds were the surgical hospitals, which were located in forward positions and handled severe trauma cases on an emergency basis. These hospitals seldom accommodated more than 60 patients at a time. Evacuation hospitals were more common, much larger, and capable of handling a census of over 300 patients simultaneously. Their primary purpose was to stabilize wounded, injured, and sick soldiers before shipping them out to American-run hospitals in Okinawa, Japan, the Philippines, or, in some cases, the United States. Finally, there were five field hospitals and one convalescent hospital. These facilities were equipped to provide long-term care and would often redeploy troops to the field after they had achieved an adequate degree of recovery. The Sixth Convalescent Hospital at Cam Ranh Bay was, by far, the largest and most elaborate hospital in Vietnam with a capacity of over 1,300 patients.

The medical care received by American troops in Vietnam was vastly superior to any care ever offered in support of military operations during time of war. The death rate from booby traps, mines, shrapnel, and other combat wounds in Southeast Asia was 19 percent but for those fortunate enough to reach a hospital alive, the mortality rate plunged to just 2.6 percent. Rapid helicopter evacuation ensured that most wounded soldiers would be under a doctor's care and in an American-run hospital within two hours of injury. The likelihood of surviving a catastrophic injury with permanent disability, however, increased correspondingly.

In May 1967, the 2nd Surgical Hospital was transferred from its location at An Khe to Chu Lai under orders to establish a semipermanent hospital compound to support the ongoing operations then being conducted by Task Force Oregon which consisted of the 11th, 196th, and 198th Infantry Brigades. The 54th Medical Detachment was similarly deployed that September to provide helicopter medical evacuation [dust-off] operations.

The placement of the new hospital facilities at Chu Lai on the Ky Ha peninsula allowed medevac helicopters to approach from the sea unimpeded by other air traffic from airbase. The hospital was, in fact, erected upon an impressive bluff with a panoramic vista of the South China Sea but its geographic proximity to two viable and tempting military targets, the Americal Division headquarters and the Marine airbase, put the hospital at increased risk of random attack by the enemy's new 122-mm rockets. Indeed, within a few months of deployment, hospital personnel cynically began to refer to their Chu Lai location as the "rocket pocket."

The 2nd Surgical Hospital was constructed from the remnants of an earlier, small Naval hospital. Cement, plywood, sand, and tin served as the primary building materials with a series of white Quonset hut structures making up the main medical wards, operating rooms, pharmacy, and labs. All were built with corrugated tin weighted down with sandbags to keep them from being torn off during the monsoon and typhoon seasons. A large red cross was carefully painted on each to identify them as peaceful medical facilities although such symbols did little to protect the hospital from enemy rocket attacks. Nearby were several portable, air-conditioned trailers which were brought in to house the commanding officer and chief nurse. Two BOQs were constructed near the compound's Officer's Club to accommodate the remaining commissioned medical personnel while four, two-story buildings quartered the hospital's enlisted staff. Sandbag covered bunkers were also strategically located throughout the hospital area to provide a degree of safety in the event of enemy attack. When vacant, these bunkers served as home to Chu Lai's ever-increasing rat colony.

In the center of the 2nd Surgical Hospital compound was the mess hall, a large facility responsible for daily feeding of the entire hospital staff, the patients, and the support personnel. A primitive movie screen fabricated from four 4-feet-by-8-feet pieces of painted plywood was erected just outside the dining area to provide entertainment for the doctors, nurses, corpsmen, and ambulatory patients. Two water towers, a helicopter landing pad, a small chapel, and a headquarters building completed the main part of the hospital compound. Several pine trees were planted near the headquarters building in an admirable but feeble effort to beautify the facilities.

By the summer of 1967, the entire system was functioning as designed, providing first-class medical care to the soldiers of the American Division and to local villagers who were often wounded in the war being waged just a few kilometers outside the Chu Lai perimeter.

A view of the Chu Lai hospital facilities looking westward from over the South China Sea. The base's helipad was immediately adjacent to the R&E. To the south was a U.S. Marine airbase while just to the north was the headquarters for the Americal Division.

For the members of the 312th Evacuation Hospital, the four weeks provided by the government putting their affairs in order before mobilization proved all too short. Employers had to be asked to hold jobs and creditors to defer bills. Families likewise had to be comforted and encouraged to maintain a stoic demeanor as each soldier prepared for what promised to be a prolonged absence away from home.

Captain Jack Medlin was one of the 312th's officers charged with achieving an orderly deployment. He was well aware that the unit was well-trained and professional, but also that it was seriously short-staffed. The U.S. Army slated the typical evacuation hospital at 300 medical and support personnel including 57 nursing positions, but the Winston-Salem unit consisted of only 209 men and 4 women reservists. The serious discrepancy in staff would have to be made up in Vietnam by transferring other U.S. Army doctors and nurses to the 312th.

On Monday, May 13, the soldiers assembled as ordered at the U.S. Army Reserve Center on Stadium Drive in Winston-Salem. Although a departure ceremony had been hastily arranged, most of the local community was oblivious to the event, being busy with the routine of daily life and enjoying the benefits of a warm, sunny spring day. For the soldiers and their families, however, little could be done to lessen the pain of this depressing and excruciating departure.

The commanding officer of the 312th, Lieutenant Colonel Eston Caldwell, attempted to place the event in perspective. He told the assemblage, "Our mission is a noble one. We must do our very best to take care of our sick and wounded fighting men." The mayor of Winston-Salem, M. C. Benton, also spoke. "The standard achieved by your unit is one of the reasons you were chosen. It is one of the penalties of youth. But we feel more comfortable having you back in our defense . . . All of our prayers should be directed to those who are negotiating today [for peace in Vietnam]."

At the conclusion of the brief ceremonies and with the Parkland High School Band playing, the soldiers of the 312th Evacuation

Hospital said a final good-bye to their loved ones. They left as a unit for Fort Benning, Georgia, where they would receive an additional 17 weeks of training before being shipped overseas to Vietnam.

Sharon left Fort Sam Houston during the afternoon of June 14. She had enjoyed her basic training and short time in San Antonio but already found herself missing her two closest friends, Janice and Barbara. The trip to her new duty station near Denver required two days of steady driving. While she was passing through New Mexico, however, an overzealous state trooper with lights flashing and siren blaring pulled her over, suspicious of the fully packed Corvair and its young occupant. After questioning her for several minutes and carefully reviewing her driver's license, car registration, and military identification card, the trooper became convinced that Sharon was not a suspected teenage runaway but, in fact, a 24-year-old commissioned officer. With a slightly embarrassed apology, he allowed her to continue on her way.

Fitzsimons Army Hospital was a large medical facility located in Aurora, Colorado, just a few miles outside Denver along Route 40. There was no real military post nor were any troops actually stationed there. In many ways, it resembled Canton's Aultman Hospital except that it was staffed primarily by military personnel rather than civilians.

After reporting to the on-duty officer that Sunday, Sharon received her housing assignment, Apartment 723-D located on West Bruns Avenue. It was conveniently located just a short distance from the main hospital complex and directly across the street from the tuberculosis wards. Still, all of the newly assigned nurses were cautioned by base personnel to keep their apartment doors locked and to drive the short distance to the hospital when working nights for their own safety and well-being.

The housing arrangements were far superior to the communal quarters in Texas and afforded a good deal of privacy. Everyone

U.S. ARMY

Fitzsimons Army Hospital in Denver, Colorado. Sharon was stationed here immediately after completing her Army training at Fort Sam Houston. Her initial assignment was in the tuberculosis wards but she was later transferred to the hospital's ICU.

KAY LANE

Sharon Lane receiving congratulations from General B. Stiger on her promotion to 2nd Lieutenant on August 30, 1968. Still, Sharon found work at the hospital to be routine and unsatisfying and after a few months, requested a transfer to Vietnam.

was assigned a roommate during their tour of duty at Fitzsimons, but the billeting office typically made little effort to accommodate differing personalities and lifestyles.

Sharon's modest second-story apartment had two bedrooms, some spartan furniture, a small living room, and an adequate kitchen. The carpets were well-worn and dirty while the orange drapes provided by the military defied good taste. A clothes washer and two dryers were located in the apartment complex's basement for the convenience of residents. It would take several weeks before Sharon and her roommate were able to make the apartment more habitable by decorating it to their own personal taste.

The next day, June 17, Sharon formally reported for duty and began routine processing. She filled out the usual amount of paperwork and got a series of shots and a preliminary dental examination. She was classified "Class I," that is in need of immediate dental care. Her first follow-up visit was scheduled for two weeks later. Finally, after several hours, she received her primary nursing assignment. To her surprise and dismay, she was detailed to begin work immediately in the hospital's tuberculosis wards, isolation units intentionally located well away from the main building because of the contagious nature of the disease. There were three wards serving such patients, two male and one female; most of these patients had contracted the disease while on military duty in Korea or other parts of Asia.

When Sharon began to work in the tuberculosis section of the hospital that June, roughly 100 men were confined in the two male wards. The majority were young, energetic, hormonal, and universally frustrated by their confinement. There were many fistfights and arguments among the patients; they were continually attempting to go AWOL [absent without official leave]. Much of the nurses' day was devoted to just trying to account for all the patients by conducting bed checks and head-counts. It was both a ridiculous and frustrating situation. Sharon felt ". . . just like a matron in a boys' school, instead of a nurse. It's almost as far from nursing as one could get working supposedly as a nurse."

To make matters even worse, the young soldiers consistently ignored the serious implications of their acute respiratory condition by continuing to smoke cigarettes and even drink. Indeed, they had become quite adept at smuggling contraband alcohol into the wards. Sharon observed, "Last Sunday night, five patients on the one men's ward smuggled in a case of beer and got plastered upstairs in this one guy's room. They broke three windows, burned the bed linen with cigarette ashes, etc. They got very belligerent with the nurse on duty and she had to call the MP's." On another occasion, a male tuberculosis patient was found passed out drunk in the parking lot with a slashed arm after he had apparently run it through a window during a downtown drinking binge.

The problems on the tuberculosis wards got progressively worse. In January, two months after Sharon had been transferred to the main hospital, a patient was found dead in his bed, apparently murdered. A weapon was found stashed nearby, and an autopsy was conducted to determine the exact cause of death. The scandal became the primary topic of discussion at Fitzsimons for several days. The results of the subsequent military investigation remained a closely guarded secret; the hospital staff never learned who was responsible for the slaying nor the motive behind it.

Sharon quickly grew dissatisfied with her nursing situation at the hospital. It was almost as if she had returned to the same life she had so desperately attempted to leave back in Ohio. In a letter to her friend Doris Plastow, she confided, "I am lonely here so far since I don't know anyone except my roommate. Sure miss the kids from Fort Sam." To make matters even worse, her roommate situation deteriorated swiftly because of continuing personality conflicts and differing values. Sharon ultimately roomed with two different people during her time in Colorado, but neither women ever became a trusted friend.

On July 7, 1968, Sharon quietly celebrated her 25th birthday. It was her first birthday away from home, friends, and family. The occasion was marked simply with a homemade supper, a far cry from the traditional, annual family gathering back in Canton. Sharon wrote, "Last night, [my roommate] cooked my birthday supper—rigatoni with sauce and those little wieners. Also she bought an individual lemon tart for each of us. We were both so full by dessert-time that we split one tart and took the other one downstairs to one of the guys who lives down there . . . I could only eat about three bites on my half-tart so I put the rest of it in the refrigerator for later."

The rigors of U.S. Army life were proving difficult as well. Although Sharon personally liked Colonel Ayers, the ranking officer-in-charge, the nurse-majors who were her immediate supervisors were careerists, who demanded that their staff abide by strict military procedures and protocol. Their authoritarian nature, infatuation with rank, and emphasis on what seemed to be trivialities made nursing at Fitzsimons even more unpleasant. "If you are dumb enough to come into the Army," Sharon paraphrased the majors lecturing the hospital staff, "you *will* take *all* I can hand out."

She had initially joined the U.S. Army as a way to exert her independence and find a different life outside of Canton but, by now, Sharon was homesick and beginning to regret her decision. "As I have said before, I am glad that I left home and am on my own now," Sharon wrote to Doris Plastow, but she expressed concern that she still had 16 months to go on her enlistment, which seemed to be an eternity. There was little that she could do personally to improve her situation. She and the other nurses frequently joked that the only way to get a discharge from the Army was to get pregnant, but that was obviously neither a viable nor a practical option.

Despite these serious misgivings, Sharon was promoted on schedule to 1st Lieutenant on August 30. She received her new silver bars from General B. Stiger in a brief commissioning ceremony along with a dentist who made lieutenant colonel and two doctors who were promoted to major. Her new rank was still a small conciliation, but it did little to alleviate her overwhelming feelings of discontent.

During this early period at Fitzsimons, Sharon repeatedly petitioned her immediate superiors for reassignment away from the tuberculosis wards, but her requests were either rejected or simply ignored. She was finally granted some much-needed leave time in late September and used the opportunity to purchase a $50 airline ticket to fly back home to Canton via Chicago. The prospect of returning home for the first time in five months was made even more exciting since it would be the first time that Sharon had ever flown on a commercial airplane.

Her visit to Canton with family and friends was brief but helped rejuvenate Sharon's sagging spirits. She was surprised, however, to find that her father quietly remained concerned about her overall well-being. "Honestly, since I left home," she wrote, "[my dad] has worried more than my mom . . . never thought he would either."

Sharon returned after her leave to Fitzsimons in mid-October and arrived to Denver's first snowfall of the season. She was excited and relieved to find that the transfer she had so desperately been seeking away from the tuberculosis wards had finally been approved. She was now assigned to the main hospital's Intensive Care Unit (ICU).

The ICU at Fitzsimons was divided into sections—cardiac patients, medical/surgical intensive care, and recovery. It was far more interesting and serious nursing, but it proved to be more intense and emotionally taxing. Open-heart surgery, a specialty at the hospital, was nevertheless risky, and many of the patients who had valve replacements and other delicate procedures died or arrested. One of the most distressing cases for Sharon and the other staff was that of a 5-year-old little girl who had been suffering from long-term multiple heart defects and who, despite their best efforts, did not survive her surgery.

Sharon had to deal with many other equally sad cases during her tenure in the ICU. One case involved a teenage girl who, in an apparent bout of depression, had poured gasoline over herself and ignited it in a suicide attempt. She suffered second and third-degree burns over much of her body, and later, a strong sense of remorse. Another time, an 11-month-old infant was briefly in Sharon's care after having emergency surgery to repair a perforated intestine caused when the child inadvertently swallowed a pair of hair-clippers. Most patients, however, were just nameless faces. Each

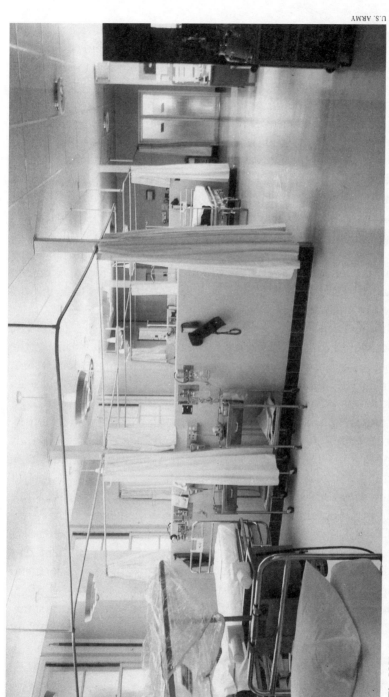

The ICU ward at Fitzsimons Hospital. Sharon spent most of her time at the hospital working on this ward. Shortly after her death, it was renamed in her honor.

day was rapidly becoming a blur of burn cases, stroke victims, heart attacks, and patients with other life-threatening conditions.

Along with the standard shifts in the ICU, Sharon and the other nurses at Fitzsimons were regularly on call to assist with routine air-evacuation. Some of the incoming patients were casualties from Vietnam, hoping to recover in a hospital near their homes; but most were simply regular GIs who required specialized treatment that could be better accommodated at other military hospitals. In November, Sharon was assigned to escort a comatose patient by ambulance to nearby Buckley Field where he was scheduled to be airlifted by military plane to a U.S. Army facility in Long Beach, California. After he had been successfully loaded onboard, Sharon then took charge of an incoming patient who was being transferred to Fitzsimons for care. He was a young private in traction who had sustained a broken neck in a car accident just prior to being deployed to Vietnam.

Sharon found that her medical schedule was relentless. The nurses were expected to work up to six days per week whenever the hospital was shorthanded, which seemed a frequent occurrence. Furthermore, the normal shifts were always rotating, so that each week it was possible to be working an odd combinations of days, afternoons, and nights without ever being able to establish a routine. Sharon complained, "I've never worked in a place where they change your time schedule so often. You just can't count on anything."

Her social life did begin to improve, albeit temporarily, while living in Colorado. For a while, she dated a lieutenant from Michigan, but it never developed into a serious relationship, being hindered by his hard partying and confirmed lack of commitment. She would also go out casually with some of the guys from her apartment complex for dinner and a few drinks. During the fall of 1968, Sharon became completely infatuated with a young, handsome, U.S. Army medic who was finishing out his military commitment after completing his required year of service in Vietnam. The U.S. Army, however, had a strict proscription against officers fraternizing with enlisted personnel and their relationship never progressed beyond some harmless flirting. She confided, though, to one of her friends, "I must tell you about this enlisted guy I have a terrible crush on. He works on one of the TB wards, is about 6′3″ . . . black hair, dark eyes. He is a medic and is from southern California originally. Also has a 'GTO' . . . He gets discharged in December '68, put in his year in Viet Nam as a field medic and was stationed in South America before that. He is very, very good since being in Viet [Nam] where they do just about *everything*. He kids me all of the time about being the *worst* Army nurse, the youngest-looking Army nurse, and the most *naive* Army nurse he has ever seen. He says I should work in the Chaplain's Office. When I work with him I absolutely cannot think straight. Of course, I'm not allowed to date him. . . ."

The dating scene was intermittent, and Sharon still spent much of her limited spare time alone in her apartment since she and her roommate continued to go their separate ways. She purchased a small, 11-inch black and white television from the local Penney's department store. Whenever her schedule permitted, she enjoyed staying up late to watch the "Tonight Show" with Johnny Carson or, on Monday evenings, she tried to set aside time for the new hit program, "Rowan and Martin's Laugh-in." She still loved to listen to records and often played them late at night on the apartment's portable stereo set. She purchased several albums from the hospital's PX, including recordings by Ray Charles, Aretha Franklin, and the Mills Brothers. Two of her favorite songs during 1968 were Glenn Campbell's hit, "By the Time I Get to Phoenix," and the Cowsills' "Indian Lake."

The time continued to drag by, and U.S. Army life at Fitzsimons had become tedious. "I'm not going out with anyone or going *anywhere* except to work so I'm slowly losing my mind," Sharon wrote on one occasion. She soon began to seriously consider putting in for a transfer to another Army medical facility. Initially, a post in West Germany seemed to be a promising option, but she was quickly dissuaded by one of her patients who told her about the country's long, cold, and wet winters and its growing anti-Americanism. She wrote, "I have decided against putting in for

Germany. We get a lot of patients on TB service from Germany and
Korea. I always ask them how they liked Germany and most say
that they hated it there. The last lady came from there about three
weeks ago. She said it was cold over there all the time. The pictures
she had with her that were taken in July '68 were taken outside on
a normal day and everyone had a coat on! . . . She never got used
to the cold, damp climate there. Also, some of them have said that
the Germans are unfriendly."

In the autumn of 1968, 20 of her fellow nurses at Fitzsimons
received their orders for Vietnam. Sharon quickly concluded that
she, too, would be happier in Southeast Asia. She wrote, "[I have
decided to] put in for Vietnam. There, at least, you are busy 12
hours a day, six or seven days a week, and you learn everything.
No time for static from majors. They don't go." At last, it would
be an opportunity to do something meaningful and significant.

Despite the frightening prospect of being sent into a war zone
during the height of hostilities, U.S. Army nurses, in general, felt
they would be relatively safe while serving in Vietnam. Indeed,
most of the American hospitals (with a few notable exceptions) were
in reasonably secure areas and, in any event, they would not be the
primary targets of a planned enemy attack. Still, it was common
knowledge among active-duty military personnel that there had already been nurse casualties during the war. The first incident had
occurred in December 1964, when four U.S. Navy nurses were
wounded in a VC terrorist bombing of an American BOQ in downtown Saigon. Although none of the women were killed, all were
awarded Purple Hearts and they performed heroically in tending to
the other casualties. Then in February 1966, two Army nurses, a
doctor, and several others were killed while passengers in a UH-1B
helicopter that crashed some 10 miles northeast of Saigon. The
chopper, piloted by one of the nurse's fiancé, was flying too low
and struck some power lines. All on-board were killed. An Army
news release tersely reported, "The two nurses were the first American servicewomen casualties in Vietnam. Both were 22, and were
on two-years of active duty following participation in the Army
Student Nurse Program." Just a few months later, two more nurses

were killed in yet another aviation accident as they were returning on a C-47 transport to hospitals in Qui Nhon.

In 1968, a U.S. Army nurse at the 85th Field Hospital became the fifth nurse to die in Vietnam. Her death was caused by complications resulting from a self-inflicted overdose of glutethimide in an apparent suicide attempt. The official Report of Casualty listed the cause of death as ". . . pneumonia secondary to an overdose of barbiturates. Self-destruction while mentally unsound." In August, Lieutenant Colonel Annie Ruth Graham, a 52-year old World War II veteran who was serving as the chief nurse at the 91st Evacuation Hospital in Tuy Hoa, suffered a major stroke. She was evacuated by air to a hospital in Japan where she died a short time later. None of these nurse casualties, though, had come as a result of any enemy action, and it was easy to dismiss each case as an isolated and unusual occurrence. Certainly there was nothing about them to deter anyone from volunteering for service in Vietnam.

The first step for Sharon to secure her transfer to Vietnam was to terminate her ongoing dental and orthodontic work. She had already had a series of X rays, dental impressions, fillings, and crowns during her almost weekly visits to the dentist, but completing the remaining procedures would require a minimum of several more months of treatment at Fitzsimons, something she was no longer willing to do.

On November 5, Richard M. Nixon was elected the nation's 37th president. Sharon was somewhat disappointed with the election returns, having supported Hubert Humphrey, but her greater concern still remained the status of her transfer orders. "I'm still waiting for my over-seas orders," she wrote. "It shouldn't be more than a couple of more months, I *hope*!!"

Sharon had to work a shift in the ICU ward a few weeks later on Thanksgiving day. Her duty roster showed that she was also scheduled to work the Christmas holiday as well. So in early December, still without word on her fate from the U.S. Army brass, Sharon decided to surprise her parents by flying home to Ohio unannounced. Immediately after completing a Sunday afternoon shift in the ICU, she caught a plane from Denver and finally called her parents during a layover between planes at Chicago's O'Hare Airport. She arrived back home in Canton during the early Monday morning hours of December 9. The entire family was thrilled by this unexpected visit and hastily gathered together that evening to celebrate an early holiday supper. Sharon, her sister, and her mother spent part of their time baking cookies and making candy together. It was a festive occasion, but altogether too short for Sharon had to return to Colorado less than 48 hours after she had arrived.

Two weeks later, on December 25, Sharon was again tending to patients on the ICU ward. The Red Cross had kindly donated small Christmas trees and poinsettias to help decorate the hospital's nursing stations and medical wards for the holiday season. The Fitzsimon's kitchen staff even prepared a special dinner of turkey, roast beef, and pecan pie for the entire staff and their captive patients. After she had finished work, Sharon called her parents to wish them a "Merry Christmas," although it took well over an hour to get through because of the high volume of holiday telephone traffic. She then went back to her apartment where she and her roommate celebrated the season quietly together. She wrote, ". . . Linda and I had a four-pound turkey I got at the commissary (Linda kept insisting that it was a *chicken*, but it wasn't). It was real good— although a little overdone . . . We haven't yet cut the pumpkin pie I got for dessert yet." The next Christmas season, Sharon fully expected to spend in the Republic of Vietnam serving with a U.S. Army hospital detachment .

A few days later, Sharon received unofficial notification that her transfer to Vietnam had been approved. The formal orders would not be cut and cleared until early January but Sharon was excited and relieved to know that her time in Colorado was now limited. She could hardly wait to leave, "Finally got my overseas orders! Am going to Viet Nam in April. Next week, however, I'm going to see our Chief Nurse, Col. Ayer, to see if I can get my date moved up so I can go sooner. Another girl who also got orders managed to get hers changed so she didn't have to go as soon, so I should be able to get changed the other way, I hope!"

When her longtime friend and former high school classmate, Doris Plastow, learned of Sharon's intentions, she was stunned and immediately wrote to her questioning the wisdom of going to Vietnam. Sharon was perplexed at Doris's reaction and promptly wrote back, "No, I haven't lost my mind. Why do you think I have? Because of putting in for Viet Nam? I'm sure looking forward to leaving *here* and to going to a warm place."

Sharon began immediately to make plans for her impending departure. She received a letter of welcome from the nurse commander in Vietnam, which included a suggested list of necessities to bring. Sharon quickly took inventory of her belongings and then began to assemble a wardrobe that would be suitable for the tropical weather of Southeast Asia. She wrote, "Went shopping this afternoon and bought a coulotte dress to take to 'Nam. Have two now. Am not planning to take many civilian clothes though because about the only place you can get to wear them is when you go on 'R & R' (Rest and Recreation). I think I would like to go to Australia on 'R & R.' Have to get a pair of sandals yet and a new watch. Mine hasn't been running well lately. Everyone says though to wait and buy a watch over there, you can get them much cheaper."

About the same time, a letter arrived at the hospital from a former nurse supervisor that was addressed to the entire staff. Sharon eagerly read the letter in anticipation of her own transfer, "We got a letter from our old supervisor, Colonel Casey, who left Fitz about six weeks ago, and she has arrived in Nam. She is out in the "boonies" at the 18th surgical hospital, which is a *MUST* unit. That is one of those transportable hospitals under tent that stays just behind the front lines. Her plane trip over the took *22* hours. She didn't say much more than that."

In early March, Sharon went down to the hospital's personnel office to begin her initial processing for departure. This procedure entailed applying for a port call date. It was estimated then that she could depart Fitzsimons around April 6, Easter Sunday. Two weeks of leave would be allotted for Sharon to put her affairs in order. Then, she would have two days travel time to reach San Francisco for overseas deployment.

Sharon's black Corvair. In April 1969, Kay Lane flew out to Denver to help her daughter move her belongings back to Canton before Sharon's deployment to Vietnam.

KAY LANE

When the time to leave finally arrived, Sharon's mother, Kay, flew out to Colorado to help her daughter pack and to accompany her on the long drive back to Ohio. Sharon had rented a U-Haul trailer for her belongings to tow behind her Corvair. It proved so big that, after she had picked up her mother at the airport, the parking lot attendant had to manually hold up the automatic gate to allow both the car and trailer to get through.

The trip back home to Canton took two days and was made a little longer by an unanticipated four-hour layover in Omaha, Nebraska, to once again repair the car. After almost a year away, Sharon was finally back home with her family. She was scheduled, however, to report to Travis Air Force base on April 24 for a flight to Long Binh, Vietnam.

5

The 312th Evac—Chu Lai, RVN

"The bombing halt the President asked for is really working. We flew over the Ho Chi Minh Trail and nothing was moving. It was the biggest traffic jam I ever saw!"
—Bob Hope, Chu Lai (December 24, 1968)

While Sharon was still stationed in Denver, three massive, U.S. Air Force C-141 Starlifter transport planes were carrying the members of the 312th Evacuation Hospital from Fort Benning, Georgia, directly to Vietnam. The long, loud, tedious, and uncomfortable flight was made only slightly more tolerable by refueling stops in Alaska and Japan where the troops had the opportunity to deplane briefly. After 26 hours of continuous travel time, they finally landed at the Marine airbase in Chu Lai, an event that was only casually acknowledged in the official logbook of the 44th Medical Brigade Headquarters for September 23 with the notation, "Summary: Arrival of the 312th Hospital."

The 312th Evacuation Hospital had already achieved considerable fame by the time it reached Vietnam as the only medical unit to have been activated by President Johnson's April call-up of the reserves. The hospital possessed a rare degree of cohesion since virtually the entire staff knew one another as friends, neighbors, and coworkers back in Winston-Salem and by having regularly trained together for years. They exhibited a good deal of "Tar Heel" pride as promptly illustrated by the impressive number of North Carolina flags that suddenly appeared throughout the Chu Lai medical wards. Even the state's renowned senator, Sam Ervin, maintained a keen interest in the unit and was kept informed through weekly correspondence with one of the 312th's higher ranking nurses and anesthetist, Major Pauline Hester.

Despite the many obvious advantages of having a well-integrated and close-knit staff working at a medical hospital in Vietnam, the 312th nevertheless posed some serious logistical problems for the U.S. Army. While replacing the 2nd Surgical Hospital which was being redeployed to Lhi Khe, a location further to the south toward the Cambodian border, the entire North Carolina hospital was scheduled to shut down operations and depart Vietnam en mass in just 12 months, effectively leaving the Chu Lai area without an operational evacuation hospital. Since no further activation of the reserves was anticipated, the U.S. Army decided to transfer several of the 312th's enlisted staff to other hospitals throughout the Republic of Vietnam. They were replaced with regular U.S. Army personnel along with the addition of several new doctors and nurses (known as the augmentation staff) in an effort to bring the 312th up to its allocated strength. These significant personnel changes meant that, ultimately, about one-third of the staff at the 312th was new to the unit. The policy did have merit, though, since it ensured a degree of continuity at Chu Lai; these individuals would be regularly rotated at varying intervals as their individual tours expired so that everyone would not be leaving Vietnam at exactly the same time. For a while, there was some minor grumbling at the 312th over the transfer of friends and colleagues. Most of the hospital remained intact, however, and it was proudly able to retain much of its southern character and charm.

The Army had allotted just seven days for the transition between the arrival of the 312th and the departure of the 2nd Surgical Hospital, a time that passed quite rapidly. On Sunday, September 29, the Commanding General of the 44th Medical Brigade arrived in

Chu Lai to formally welcome the reservists to Vietnam. The unit became fully operational just two days later on October 1.

The 312th Evacuation Hospital was a marvel of American efficiency and technology. Its well-engineered design was intended to maximize the hospital's effectiveness with its labs, pharmacy, central supply, preop, X ray, and surgical buildings all located in close proximity. Most importantly, the entrance to the Receiving and Emergency (R&E) area was contiguous with the hospital's helipad which meant that the incoming wounded could be off-loaded and under medical care within seconds of landing. Ample supplies of blood, narcotics, bandages, and other medical necessities were neatly stockpiled nearby and readily available to meet any possible emergency.

The hospital's medical staff, after having been augmented by transfers and finally assembled in Chu Lai, would have been the envy of any modern, stateside urban facility. The 312th had a talented group of physicians who individually specialized in orthopedic, ophthalmologic, vascular, and oral surgery all of whom had just completed outstanding residency programs and were fully conversant with the latest medical and surgical techniques. In addition, the 378th Medical Detachment, a fully mobile neurosurgery unit, was assigned full time to the Chu Lai hospital complete with its allotment of two neurosurgeons—doctors Michael Carey and Jacob Mathias—an anesthesiologist (James Kryvicky), a nurse, and three corpsmen. Finally, there were several General Medical Officers (GMOs) who were equivalent to general practitioners in the United States.

The U.S. Army was remarkably adept at maintaining an adequate supply of doctors during the war although there were occasional shortages of individual specialties. The selective service system, adopted in the United States primarily to feed the nation's need for fighting men, actually worked quite well in obtaining doctors for service in Vietnam. The law provided that any medical student who had accepted a college deferment would be required to remain eligible for the draft until the age of 34. Likewise, a companion program, known as the "Barry Plan," enabled young doctors to com-

The headquarters building at the 312th Evacuation Hospital. The reserve unit from Winston-Salem, North Carolina, was activated in April 1968 and began hospital operations in Chu Lai, RVN, on October 1st.

plete their internship training and residency requirements uninterrupted in return for two years active service.

With the Vietnam War at its peak in 1968, American forces were sustaining their largest numbers of casualties, weekly averaging 500 killed and over 3,000 wounded. From the very beginning of their tours, dust-off choppers arrived continually at the 312th Evacuation Hospital, each carrying a fresh cargo of the injured and wounded.

The hospital's R&E became the center of emergency medical activity; it was a busy and bloody place. A series of metal sawhorses were set up just inside the main facility to support the stretchers of the incoming wounded. During mass casualty situations, the unit's doctors and nurses undertook the grim business of sorting through the injured, categorizing each soldier according to the severity of his wounds. To the uninitiated, this triage procedure was callous and cruel, but it was an unavoidable necessity during time of war. Indeed, with most of the wounded patients suffering from severe trauma and requiring multiple surgical procedures, it was impera-tive to assign treatment based upon need to make maximum use of the hospital's finite resources and manpower. Some required im-mediate medical intervention while others could have treatment delayed or needed only a minimal amount of care. Those cases that were hopeless were classified as expectants and usually involved catastrophic head traumas and were, in the words of one 312th R&E nurse, ". . . non-responsive, decerebrate (having a body posture with the limbs being rigid, extended), with pupils fixed and dilated. These wounds were obviously fatal. The patients would not live through surgery, let alone recover." The expectants were moved to the rear of the R&E while the staff was involved in treating other casualties and gradually, these dreadfully injured soldiers slipped away mercifully into death.

Top priority was given to soldiers who, although severely wounded, could be saved through immediate medical intervention. These men were quickly treated; airways were assured with an endotrachael [wind pipe] tube if needed and bleeding was stopped while intervenous fluids were started with large gauge needles. Once medically stabilized, the wounded were X rayed, brought to preop,

DR. MICHAEL CAREY

Doctors and nurses work on a patient in the 312th's R&E. Metal sawhorses were used to support stretchers while medical personnel worked rapidly to determine the nature and severity of each patient's wounds.

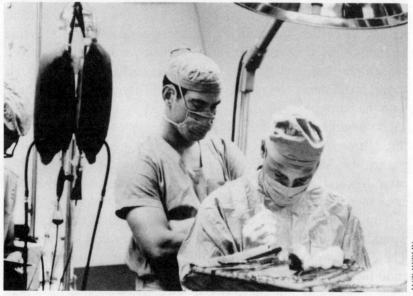

JACK MEDLIN

Two doctors prepare for surgery. The 312th had an outstanding staff of doctors and nurses who provided first class medical treatment to the sick, injured, and wounded.

and then to surgery as quickly as their condition dictated. Patients with non life-threatening wounds were treated next whenever the hospital staff was free to care for them, X rayed and then brought to the pre-operative holding area or to the operating room.

The human residue of modern war was shocking to even the most experienced medical personnel. In the single year that the doctors and nurses were stationed in Vietnam, they handled more amputations, head injuries, gunshot wounds, and exotic diseases than they would see at that time in a lifetime of medical practice in the United States. 1st Lieutenant Mary Mentzger, a young nurse from Columbus, Ohio, volunteered to go to Vietnam shortly after completing nursing school. She vividly recalled her own abrupt introduction to trauma cases at Chu Lai's R&E. As she was undergoing her routine orientation at the hospital shortly after reporting for duty, a medevac helicopter radioed that it would be arriving shortly with a casualty. Almost simultaneously, the roar of helicopter blades drowned out all other sounds as several corpsmen raced through a blinding cloud of dust to the hospital's helipad. Moments later, they returned with a stretcher bearing a severely wounded GI. It was obvious that he was a muscular, well-built man over six feet tall, but his features were totally obscured by blood, dirt, and sweat. He was already in serious distress and having profound difficulty breathing. With each gasp for breath, he inhaled instead more of his own blood so that he was literally choking and drowning in his own fluids. In a panic, he began to thrash about wildly, fear evident in his eyes, while four male corpsmen physically restrained him. One of the hospital doctors quickly performed an emergency tracheotomy while other hospital staff cut away the soldier's clothes and started an IV of saline solution to reverse shock. Finally able to breath, the patient calmed down and was quickly carried off into surgery. The whole incident, in what seemed to be almost a choreographed stage play, had lasted just a few minutes. Later that day, Lieutenant Mentzger encountered the same soldier in the ICU, now anesthetized, medicated, bandaged, and well on his way to recovery. For the hospital, it was just another routine case, but the results had nevertheless been nothing short of miraculous.

The stress and intensity pervasive in the atmosphere of the 312th's R&E only increased with word of any new offensive action being conducted by the neighboring Americal Division which was responsible for operations in some of the least pacified territory in Vietnam. Inevitably, their offensives produced many casualties which would challenge and strain the 312th's personnel and resources.

In a war zone, however, the unexpected often became the norm. Ironically, one of the worst days for casualties at the 312th occurred when there was little fighting. A Fairchild C-123 propeller-driven transport plane loaded with GIs en route home, crashed shortly after takeoff at the Chu Lai airfield. For the next several hours, a steady stream of patients arrived at the 312th Evacuation Hospital, most with life-threatening third-degree burns. One of the most distressing cases was that of a young, 19-year-old boy with hauntingly blue eyes. He had sustained burns over 90 percent of his body; only his feet were unscarred, having been protected from the intense flames by his combat boots. He, like most of the other passengers, later died. It was a particularly poignant time for the entire hospital staff since the crash was an accident having little to do with the war effort. Furthermore, the plane's human cargo consisted of combat soldiers and a physician who, only moments before, had been overjoyed that they had survived their one-year tours of duty and were headed home to loved ones. At the 312th, it was obvious that there were just far too many ways to die in Vietnam. As if to accent that fact, a large sign next to the helipad alerted the medical staff to proceed with caution when off-loading casualties:

DANGER
Helicopters Can Kill You.
1. Never approach from direct front or rear.
2. Keep down to five feet or lower.
3. Approach all planes' right middle section door.
Stay clear of chopper's rear.
Don't Lose Your Head—Use It

The 312th was well-equipped with eight individual operating rooms, although two of these rooms were seldom used. After surgery, the seriously wounded patients were moved to the nearby intensive care unit which was divided into two sections—one accommodating soldiers who remained in critical condition and the other reserved for surgical recovery. When possible, those who had progressed sufficiently were moved to step-down wards where those in non-critical condition were cared for and all seriously wounded patients were eventually evacuated. Initially, the men were transported by field ambulances or specially modified buses to the nearby airbase to an awaiting C-130 for the short flight to Da Nang. There they were admitted briefly to an Air Force hospital to ensure their medical stability before being flown on a specially configured Air Force C-141 to more elaborate American hospitals in Japan or the Philippines for further treatment and recovery. Finally, the soldiers were flown back to the Continental United States (CONUS). The entire process was usually initiated within five days from the time of first admission. It was not unusual for the 312th to arrange for the evacuation of up to 100 patients each day, but these casualties were inevitably replaced by more incoming sick and wounded.

Three wards at the 312th were designed primarily to receive medical cases. Malaria, dysentery, and venereal diseases were common ailments among American troops, along with a large number of cases involving "jungle rot," skin rashes, and other infections. A short confinement to the hospital for a minor medical condition was seen by many soldiers as a welcome respite from the horrors of the war since it provided them with the opportunity to rest, talk to American women, and eat hot food.

The last of the hospital wards at the 312th were reserved for Vietnamese patients. Most of the medical staff did not want to work in this area and few were ever ordered to do so. Besides the obvious problems inherent in the language barrier, many irrationally blamed the Vietnamese people for much of the pain and suffering being inflicted daily upon the American GIs. In a country where friend and foe, enemy and ally, were indistinguishable, the civilian population was seen as complicit in their support of the VC. Indeed,

U.S. soldiers on patrol were rarely warned by the peasant villagers of impending ambushes, booby traps, mines, or other danger. Consequently, they sustained numerous casualties. In reality, the Vietnamese were in an untenable situation. During the day, American and ARVN forces were in their villages demanding information and searching for the enemy while at night, the Communists controlled the countryside. The NVA and VC showed no mercy toward these poor people and would brutally torture and murder anyone who assisted the Americans. Even basic knowledge of a few English words was tantamount to a death sentence for the Vietnamese people as 20th-century war viciously descended upon a mostly illiterate, agrarian, peasant population who simply wished to be left alone.

The Vietnamese ward at Chu Lai consisted of two, identical, white Quonset hut structures connected by a short, enclosed hallway forming an H shape. In between the two buildings were the toilet and shower facilities for the patients along with a small storage area for hospital supplies. Each ward contained 22 beds; a large, Army-issue, wooden desk was located in the middle of each ward to serve as the central nursing station.

Ward 4-B was marked with a plywood sign as "The Village." A gold and red Republic of Vietnam flag was painted above the nurse's desk. Virtually all the patients on the ward were Vietnamese civilians—mostly women and children. They suffered from head injuries, amputations, and fragmentation wounds plus a variety of other non war-related injuries such as kerosene and gasoline fire burns. A few were even in need of intensive-care monitoring, but because of space limitations and the priority given to American soldiers, they could not be sent to the hospital's Intensive Care Ward.

The American medical policy toward the Vietnamese civilian population was motivated primarily by humanitarian reasons but it was also intended to help win the "hearts and minds" of the people. Not only were war injuries cared for, but also other medical ailments typical of impoverished countries were treated. The 312th doctors dealt with goiters, cleft palettes, intestinal parasites, tuberculoses, malnutrition, cerebral malaria, tetanus, and even rabies and bubonic plague. For most of the peasants, it was the only time in their lives they ever received professional medical care. In a nation of some 17 million people, there were just 7,000 professionally trained doctors. What few Vietnamese hospitals that did exist operated under difficult conditions, lacking running water, screened windows, and even basic medicines. Patients slept on plywood mattresses, which were sometimes covered with small, straw pallets. As a result, American doctors, who treated the Vietnamese patients fortunate enough to reach the 312th, often kept them longer than the normal recovery period to ensure that they were completely healed. There was no guarantee or likelihood that these patients would ever receive any further medical care. As did most U.S. Army hospitals, the 312th adopted the enlightened policy of permitting the families of their Vietnamese patients to stay in the hospital while their loved ones were being treated. These people usually slept on the floor, under a patient's bed and actually proved to be of valuable assistance to the nursing staff by helping to feed, care, and comfort the patients.

Enemy prisoners of war (POWs) were confined to the adjacent and connecting ward. Under the provisions of the 1949 Geneva Convention, these soldiers were entitled to medical care and treatment for their wounds despite the ongoing hostilities. The treaty clearly stated, "Prisoners of war suffering from serious disease, or whose condition necessitates special treatment, a surgical operation, or hospital care, must be admitted to any military or civilian medical unit where such treatment can be given . . ." As a precaution, though, an armed military policeman was posted at all times in the ward to protect both the hospital staff and other patients from potential harm. This danger was real. Both the PAVN and Viet Cong universally held a deep-rooted bitterness toward the United States and its South Vietnamese ally, and they did little to disguise their disdain. Even after receiving treatment, Viet Cong and NVA soldiers often spit on American medical personnel and anything that could conceivably be used as a weapon had to be secured and kept far away. For the medical staff of the 312th, it was the first time in their lives that they had ever personally experienced pure, unadulterated hatred directed towards them. The nurses found such animosity particularly difficult to comprehend since their stated mission in Vietnam was to help rather than to kill. In truth, the doctors and nurses were always relieved to discharge enemy prisoners to the ARVN authorities for incarceration at a POW compound for a hospital had little time for bitterness.

The 312th Evacuation Hospital was considered to be good duty, at least by Vietnam standards. As a reserve unit, the overall atmosphere at the hospital compound was more relaxed than that found at typical regular U.S. Army units. Military protocol, rank, and red tape were given a low priority, logically subordinate to the 312th's overall medical mission. Saluting at the hospital was lax; no one ever enforced the regulations requiring doctors to wear their uniforms around the hospital complex. Instead, the physicians could be routinely seen around the compound dressed in their green surgical scrubs. While not according to regulations, it was an excellent way to combat the severe heat.

The overall operational philosophy at the 312th was based on the premise that its medical staff was both professional and competent. The staff was expected to do its duty and meet their responsibilities just as they had done daily while in civilian life. Hence, there was no need to sound reveille to begin the day since the doctors, nurses, and corpsmen all could be relied upon to report for their scheduled shifts promptly to relieve their coworkers who had just completed their own marathon 12-hour rotations. Even the strict military proscription against fraternization between officers and enlisted personnel was not rigorously enforced. The entire staff ate at a communal mess hall, although it was divided into separate sections for the officers and enlisted staff. At midnight "chow," however, all hospital personnel ate together, regardless of rank. Several intense romances even developed between some of the young nurses and the enlisted corpsmen at the hospital. These relationships, although never condoned, were generally ignored as long as they were kept discreet and did not interfere with the smooth operation of the hospital.

The majority of the doctors stationed at the 312th lived in "hooches" located just a few yards from the main hospital area so they could be quickly summoned in case of emergency. These primitive, barracks-types of housing were actually remnants of the old medical wards that had served as a small, rudimentary U.S. Navy-Marine hospital in 1965 when Chu Lai was still considered a forward position. The nurses and the non-physician officers were billeted in the compound's two BOQs a bit further away from the hospital's R&E. Each person had his or her own room, spacious by Vietnam standards (roughly 8 feet by 12 feet), cooled by only a single ceiling fan, which ran continuously but could do little to alleviate the relentless heat. The exterior wall consisted entirely of mesh screening to help keep the bugs out; wooden slats were overlaid to achieve a louvered effect to increase air circulation and ensure privacy. The rooms were sparsely furnished with metal lockers serving as a closets and standard hospital beds. Sand and dirt were incessant problems while Vietnam's large assortment of bugs and insects, some of which grew to gargantuan proportions, were constant intruders. The ants were especially precocious and had an annoying habit of nesting in toothbrushes. The drab surroundings at the BOQs were made slightly more agreeable when the base commanders adopted a policy that allowed the residents to paint their individual doors. Virtually everyone exercised this right of personal expression and used the brightest and gaudiest colors available.

One of the BOQs occupied ideal real-estate near the southernmost portion of the hospital compound, next to a steep bluff that dropped dramatically off to the beach below. The seaward residents had a spectacular view of the South China Sea and of the white sand beach which extended southward some 20 miles down to the Batangay peninsula, a region which was continually under Viet Cong occupation. The other building, located directly opposite the seaward BOQ but slightly closer to the mess hall, was sarcastically named "the Chu Lai Hilton" by its inhabitants and identified by a crude, homemade sign strategically nailed to a second-floor balcony. In

A view of the H-shaped hospital wards. The toilet and shower facilities were in the center while a covered walkway linked the various wards with other parts of the hospital. The 312th's headquarters and chapel are visible in the center as is the massive mess hall.

The BOQ at the 312th looking inward toward the hospital compound and the "Chu Lai Hilton." Sharon lived in this building on the 2nd floor after stationing in Vietnam. Her room overlooked the volleyball court and bunker. Each resident attempted to express their individuality by painting their doors. Most chose bright, loud colors.

between the two structures, was a sandbagged bunker and a volley-ball court, which was in almost continuous use during off-duty hours. The shower facilities were small, inconvenient, and slippery, and they afforded little privacy. The latrines were in the process of being upgraded with the important luxury of running water for flush toilets.

The entire 312th Evacuation Hospital compound was carefully separated and isolated from the other Chu Lai military installations by a barbed wire fence. All of the unit's enlisted men, including medical corpsmen, were required to complete a regular guard duty shift. Although there was some fear of an enemy assault, the more persistent problem was with American GIs trying to gain unauthorized access to the hospital compound: These soldiers were desperate for female companionship or just anxious for some simple conversation with a "round-eyed" woman. Still, access to the hospital had to be restricted for practical reasons; no one could be allowed to interfere with its medical priorities.

The work at the 312th was continuous and grueling. The nurses, most of whom were in their early twenties, worked six individual 12-hour shifts per week with just one day off. They were under the constant stress of dealing with the injured, the maimed, and the dead. As a matter of simple survival and to retain their sanity, they lived their lives day to day; their reality was confined to the hospital wards and isolated from the political developments and the social upheavals ravaging the United States. Those rare off-duty hours not devoted to sleep were cherished moments needed to relax, decompress, and forget.

The post's Officer's Club became the center of social activity for the hospital staff. It was located conveniently adjacent to the BOQs and was cooled by a powerful 1000-Btu air conditioner, which had been originally intended for an airplane hangar but was somehow "misappropriated" to Chu Lai. The ice-cold air of the club, though, was a welcome change from the constant heat and humidity. Each day, several of the doctors and nurses would gather there to talk, write letters, and play cards. The club offered patrons a regular fare of cool drinks, beer, and music. There, it was possible to forget for a few moments that there was a war going on; that people were dying a few kilometers away in the field; and that there were patients in pain in the nearby hospital wards. Amy Lazar, a Red Cross social worker assigned to the 312th, wrote in her personal log, "The irony of the war was displayed tonight as we had a show . . . a combo played so loud no one could hear the roar of the jets, etc. While we were enjoying the music, men are out in the field fighting. WHAT A CONTRAST!! One can almost sit and watch the war as if it were a movie show and not for real."

On most evenings, there were impromptu dances at the club with a record player providing the music. These social affairs ultimately posed a serious problem, however, since all military officer's clubs were required by law to be open facilities. Officers from any unit or branch of service were entitled to access. Officers from the neighboring Americal Division and the jet pilots from the Marine airbase were, in fact, frequent visitors to the club and possessed the singular mission of meeting a pretty, young nurse. The resulting mix proved volatile and erupted into violence one evening. A 312th doctor, who was deaf in one ear, attempted to cut in on a U.S. Marine officer who was dancing with one of the hospital's staff nurses. The soldier refused to be interrupted, but the physician, unaware of the menacing tone in the man's voice spoken into his deaf ear, persisted. A fight quickly ensued with the doctor the obvious loser.

This serious altercation led to a reassessment concerning policies governing the operation of the Officer's Club. To avoid further disputes, it was renamed the "Chu Lai Medical Society" and its membership was thus restricted only to doctors and nurses stationed with the 312th. Other military officers, including those from other units, could be initiated into this closed society but only after conducting a lecture, a briefing, or a presentation to the club's active members. Talks were held on such diverse topics as the civilian pacification program, the Chu Lai air defense system, and the program for international development. This policy was designed to help facilitate better relationships with the other bases and give the medical staff a better understanding of how the war was being conducted. It also had the added benefit of eliminating most of the troublemakers. Eventually, the Chu Lai Medical Society consisted of a more restrained group, which even included Major General Charles M. Gettys, the commanding officer of the Americal Division, whose staff presented an outstanding briefing on the role of his division in Vietnam.

Other amenities were available around the Chu Lai area. Just outside the entrance to the hospital was the Post Exchange which stocked a wide variety of products: cameras, tape-recorders, food, and other necessities. To the south, the United Services Organization (USO) operated a club, which was well-stocked with the latest American magazines and even had a pool table while the Marine Air Groups also had their own outstanding officer and NCO clubs.

Still, most off-duty hours were simply devoted to catching up on lost sleep. The heat and the pungent smell of the countryside made this difficult during most months. During the monsoon season, dampness and mildew were the problems. Many of the staff who worked the night shifts would abandon their rooms to sunbathe, relax, and sleep on lounge chairs set up in a fence-enclosed patio area next to the Officer's Club. Others would walk down to the USO beach, although the presence of Vietnamese fishermen was a distraction. The numerous gun emplacements spaced at regular intervals and barbed wire served as stern reminders that they were still in a war zone.

Movies were shown at night regularly in the courtyard next to the mess hall. Four pieces of whitewashed plywood served as a makeshift screen. The films were fairly recent, usually less than a year old, but the outdoor acoustics were barely adequate. Director David Lean's epic, *Dr. Zhivago*, was one of the more popular selections, but its dramatic panoramas of the Siberian tundra seemed curiously out of place in the semitropical climate of South Vietnam. The U.S. Army even managed to procure recent films of major American sporting events including the climactic football game between the universities of Ohio State and Purdue, ranked number one nationally. The Ohio State Buckeyes won 10 to 0.

Several Hollywood celebrities visited Chu Lai while on their so-called "handshake," goodwill tours of Vietnam. Troy Donahue,

Sebastian Cabot, and Ricardo Montalban all visited the patients at the 312th Evacuation Hospital on separate occasions. Montalban, whose most recent performances at the time were in the films, *Cheyenne Autumn* and *Madam X*, was unknown to the mostly young patients and medical staff. Still, Amy Lazar, a Red Cross social worker at the 312th remembered him as ". . . a most gracious personality, a true gentlemen. He spent a great deal of time talking to each patient and [was] very sincere and concerned. He said he was most inspired by the attitude of the men and what they are doing here." Certainly the most famous celebrity to visit during the 312th's tour was Bob Hope, who brought his annual, morale-boosting Christmas show to Chu Lai on December 24, 1968.

When the U.S. Navy Seabees enlarged the Chu Lai base area, they constructed an amphitheater adjacent to the hospital for just such entertainers. The American Division was responsible for making the preparations to receive Hope and his entourage. It was assigned the code name *Operation Holly* and every effort was made to secure the surrounding area. Apparently the North Vietnamese were well aware of the visit and the impending holiday show since there was a marked increase in their activity. From December 18 through 21, the Chu Lai area was rocketed 14 times while the surrounding firebases—Landing Zones (LZ's) Snoopy, Dottie, Rawhide, Custer, Phoenix, Bronco, Cindy, *et al.*—were under a constant state of alert. Bob Hope and his traveling troupe were undaunted, however; thousands of American troops from the entire region crowded into the Special Services amphitheater to see the highly anticipated Christmas show. The stage was decorated with USO banners and two large paintings of the American division patch with its four stars on a blue background. Special consideration was given to wounded GIs from the 312th and their attending nurses and physicians. The front row was reserved for wheelchairs. Ambulatory patients, readily identifiable by their light blue pajamas, were also given priority seating for the performance.

The show was a massive undertaking and featured such luminaries as Rosie Grier, the all-pro tackle of the Los Angeles Rams, and Penelope Plummer, the newly crowned Miss World. To the troops'

USO

Actress/singer Ann-Margret performing with the Bob Hope show at Chu Lai on December 24, 1968. Soldiers from throughout the I-Corps region attended the performance. Patients from the hospital were given priority seating.

USO

Los Angeles Rams football player Rosie Grier addresses the troops at Chu Lai. The program ended with the entire cast leading the soldiers in a heart-rending rendition of "Silent Night."

delight, the vivacious and sexy Ann-Margret performed as did the 12 beautiful girls who made up the Golddiggers dancing troupe.

Bob Hope was already a legend among American troops, having performed for them during World War II, Korea, and now Vietnam. His presence and commitment were inspirations to the troops, most of whom were spending their first Christmas away from home. Hope's monologue was contemporary, funny, and, at times, poignant. He began with recounting the news of Richard M. Nixon's recent election to the presidency and the surprising marriage of Jacqueline Kennedy to Aristotle Onassis, "Everything's fine back home. Nixon captured Washington and Jackie Kennedy's got Greece . . . I know you remember Nixon, Ike's caddie. So everything's in good shape." Hope then focused his attention on the continuing domestic turmoil and campus unrest in the United States, "Actually, I'd planned to spend Christmas in the United States, but I can't stand the violence . . . Last year, the students were burning their draft cards. This year, it's the colleges. When you muster out, keep your rifle. If you want to go to school under the GI Bill," Hope joked, "you may have to capture one first."

The show's finale featured the entire cast joining Bob Hope on stage and leading the soldiers in a heartrending rendition of "Silent Night." Many in the audience and several on stage were moved to tears, remembering past Christmases back home: good times with family and friends, holiday cheer and brightly wrapped gifts, peace and goodwill toward men.

6

Twenty Hours to War

"U.S. Vietnam Dead Pass Korean War Total."
—*Life* Magazine (April 4, 1969)

The overwhelming sense of relief that Sharon Lane experienced in leaving her nursing position at Fitzsimons Hospital was quickly replaced by a growing sense of anticipation about going to Vietnam. It promised to be an exciting and interesting tour of duty—a time of meaningful nursing in an exotic country of Buddhists, pagodas, and pedicabs.

The two weeks that the Army granted Sharon in leave time before her scheduled deployment was rapidly filled with important visits to family and friends, a series of good-byes, and storing away her personal items for the year that she planned to be away from Ohio. On Wednesday evening, April 23, 1969, dressed casually in her civilian clothes, Sharon boarded a scheduled commercial flight from Canton-Akron Airport for the short trip to Chicago. The plane was delayed in a holding pattern over Gary, Indiana, however, and she arrived at O'Hare Airport barely in time to catch a departing west-bound United Airlines connection to San Francisco. With the

3-hour time difference and the actual travel time, the plane did not arrive in California until 1130 hours (Pacific Savings Time), far too late for her to make the additional 90-minute trip to Travis Air Force Base. Further complicating matters was the fact that the airline had lost Sharon's duffel bag containing all of her uniforms, clothing, and other personal items. After spending several frustrating minutes filing the appropriate lost baggage forms with United Airline's officials, she then caught a taxi into San Francisco. Exhausted and worn out from a long night of travel, she checked into a local motel shortly after midnight to the suspicious glances of the night clerk, obviously intrigued with the curious circumstances involving an attractive young woman traveling alone without any luggage.

Early the following morning, refreshed from a good night's sleep, Sharon caught another taxi to the San Francisco Greyhound bus station. There, she purchased a $2.65 one-way ticket to Fairfield, California, some 60 miles away and the home to Travis Air Force Base. The bus was crowded with other passengers and several soldiers as it left the city and crossed over the massive Oakland Bay Bridge and into Alameda County, giving Sharon a glimpse of the majestic San Francisco Bay and its famed obsolete prison, Alcatraz. Also visible from Interstate 80 was the gray university tower at Berkeley, the center of the increasingly militant anti-war movement that was sweeping through the nation's college campuses that spring much to the frustration of Governor Ronald Reagan. This urban scenery, however, soon gave way to the more monotonous, featureless terrain of northern California, interrupted at regular intervals only by fast-food restaurants, gas stations, and cheap motels.

Travis Air Force Base, nestled in the gently rolling hills of the Suison Valley, occupied some 5,266 acres of land. There were few trees in the immediate vicinity and the surrounding terrain took on an almost colorless light brown hue, occupied mainly by farms and pastures along with a few pioneering vineyards and the long airport runways of the military base. Travis was originally constructed in 1942 during the nadir days of World War II to support military operations against the Japanese in the Pacific. The facility earned the title, "Gateway to the Pacific" and evolved into a major debarkation route for deployment of US troops overseas throughout the Cold War period. By 1969, Travis was the home of the 60th Military Airlift Wing [60 MAW] and along with Norton Air Force Base in San Bernidino and McChord Air Force Base in Tacoma, virtually every American en route to Vietnam was destined to pass through one of these three facilities. That year alone, over 10,300 chartered airline flights transporting troops to and from Southeast Asia used Travis Air Force Base. During this peak period, the facility was averaging one such flight per hour, an impressive traffic volume that rivaled even some of the nation's smaller urban airports.

The Travis terminal was housed in a small, nondescript, beige and brown, one-story structure located immediately adjacent to the control tower and the flight line. Several military airmen manned stations behind the ticket counters, busily processing overseas orders and assigning flight times to the soldiers in line. In many ways, the scene resembled that of a typical, civilian airport but notably one without the usual comforts or amenities except for the fact that virtually everyone wore a military uniform.

When Sharon's bus finally arrived at Travis Air Force Base, she was surprised by the large number of soldiers who were crowded into the terminal awaiting transport to Vietnam. She also felt quite conspicuous in her inappropriate civilian attire but was relieved to discover that United Airlines recovered her missing duffel bag and had promptly delivered it to the base. She quickly changed into her regulation green cord uniform complete with low heels.

All the outbound flights from the base had been carefully scheduled to leave late at night to ensure that the flight time of more than 20 hours would be coordinated with a daytime landing in Vietnam. Sharon received a 2030 hours departure onboard a TWA 707 charter along with two other Army nurses and a woman from the Women's Army Corps. The remaining 161 seats on the flight were filled to capacity with regular infantry. TWA normally flew two such MAC-PAC transport flights each week, while World Airways, American Airlines, Continental, and a few other commercial carriers also reg-

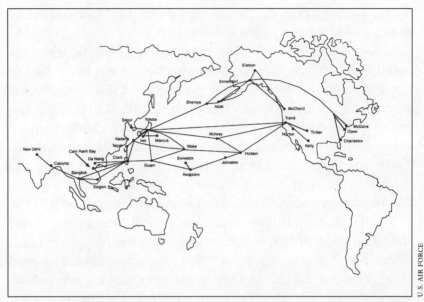

A map of the major air routes to Asia during the Vietnam War. The vast majority of Americans destined for Vietnam left from Travis, Norton, or McChord Air Force Bases.

U.S. AIR FORCE

U.S. Army soldiers boarding a World Airways plane at Travis Air Force Base. TWA, American, and other commercial charters helped provide transport during the war. Sharon left Travis on April 24, 1969, at 2030 hours on a TWA 707.

U.S. AIR FORCE

ularly provided additional military charters during this period of military buildup.

Shortly before the scheduled time for departure, Sharon made one last effort to call her parents back home in Canton for a final good-bye, but she was unable to get through. Disappointed and slightly dejected, she joined the remaining passengers on the runway's tarmac and slowly climbed the boarding ladder onto the waiting jet. Sharon and the three other women were intentionally assigned seating near the front of the aircraft to afford them some degree of privacy. The nurses quickly became friends and they chatted quietly together. Most of the troops attempted to get some sleep while the others were pensive, lost in their private thoughts, trying to anticipate the coming months. The TWA flight crew, comprised of five stewardesses and a male purser, busily served refreshments and a light meal after the plane was airborne over the Pacific Ocean. They also attempted to relieve the anxiety of their passengers and make them reasonably comfortable.

The long trip to Vietnam required the plane to make two refueling stops. The first destination along its route was Hawaii, a six-hour flight from Travis Air Force Base. Once there, for their own safety, all the passengers were required to deplane while the aircraft took on additional fuel while being serviced by civilian ground personnel. During the brief 45-minute layover, the soldiers and nurses waited tensely in Honolulu's new, modern, commercial terminal, freely mixing with vacationing tourists and young couples on a romantic holiday to this tropical paradise. It provided a dramatic and striking contrast for those whose final destination was a war zone.

When the plane was finally ready, Sharon and the rest of the soldiers reboarded for the next leg of their journey, a marathon nine-hour flight to Okinawa, Japan. The highlight of this portion of the trip occurred when the plane crossed the International Date Line; Friday miraculously dissolved into Saturday in this new, unfamiliar part of the world.

When the plane finally landed on Okinawa, it was the first stop in Asia. The island, part of the Ryukyu Island chain, had become notorious some 24 years earlier as the site of the last major battle of World War II. Thousands of American sailors and soldiers fought and died for this volcanic rock pile and braved Kamikaze attacks and a fierce defense by the Japanese army. When Okinawa was finally captured, it became a major American base in the Pacific and still remained firmly under U.S. control despite increasingly vocal protests from Tokyo.

The Okinawa airbase was in perpetual motion, serving as a major staging area for B-52 bombers and their deadly raids along the Ho Chi Minh trail and against military targets in North Vietnam. Seeing these gargantuan jets and their awesome power firsthand brought the war into sharp focus for the TWA passengers. There was a resulting appreciable increase in tension since all were well aware they were now just a short, three-hour hop away from Vietnam.

Although the final leg of their trip was by far the shortest portion of the flight, each second seemed to pass slowly as the plane relentlessly made its way over Taiwan and the South China Sea before making a final approach into Long Binh from the northeast. From her vantage point high above the country, Sharon could see little tangible evidence of the ongoing war raging below. Instead, the lush, green countryside appeared to be tranquil, neatly carved into uniform rectangular patches by hundreds of rice paddies. The deep blue seas of the coastal areas provided a startling contrast of vivid color. The experienced TWA pilot and flight crew, however, were far more attuned to the potential dangers of landing in a war zone. Strict operating procedures required the plane to maintain absolute radio silence during its final seven-minute approach into Long Binh to avoid any potential detection by enemy forces.

Just moments before landing, the plane made an abrupt, rapid, and steep decent into the airport, a precipitous maneuver known euphemistically as a "high-and-hot" approach. It was designed to minimize the risk of provoking hostile fire, but it was disconcerting even to the most seasoned of travelers. Once safely on the ground, the jet taxied hurriedly up to the Long Binh terminal. First Lieutenant Sharon A. Lane, U.S. Army Nurse Corps, and her compatriots had finally arrived in the Republic of Vietnam. It was 0800 hours, Saturday, April 26, 1969.

The TWA flight crew cheerfully bid each of their passengers good-bye and wished them all a safe tour of duty. Still, it was painfully obvious that they were anxious to service the plane and get airborne as quickly as possible. It was common knowledge that their sleek red and white jet continued to present a tempting target while stationary on the Long Binh tarmac.

As Sharon stepped out of the relative darkness of airplane and onto the boarding ladder, she was temporarily blinded by the bright early morning sunlight. Almost immediately, the brutal heat of Vietnam overwhelmed her. It was unlike anything she had ever experienced, even during the hottest of Midwestern summers back in Ohio. Indeed, the soaring temperature was exhausting and draining. It seemed to press down heavily on her, forcing sweat from virtually every pore and soaking her uniform in just a matter of seconds. The comfortable cool of the air-conditioned plane had already slipped into distant memory.

Compounding matters was the awful smell—a combination of unique aromas, all individually obnoxious, but somehow cooked by the heat and blended into a fetid alchemy that defied description. Despite the massive and obvious American military presence, Vietnam remained entrenched in a largely preindustrial society with few sanitation or sewage facilities. Human waste was burned in large cauldrons while the surrounding peasant farmers used untreated excrement as fertilizer for their fields. Also, there was *nuoc mam*, a pungent fish sauce popular with the Vietnamese but whose smell was so strong that no newly arrived American could tolerate it. Even the fragrant scents of burning incense from family ancestral shrines and Buddhist temples could do little to offset the overpowering stench.

After recovering from these initial assaults on her senses, Sharon and her traveling companions, Kathi and Rose, made their way down the ladder toward the primitive structure that was serving as the Long Binh terminal. Concertina wire, armed guards, military police, and armed aircraft were strikingly in evidence to the debarking passengers who slowly made their way past a group of anxious GIs eagerly awaiting their opportunity to board the now vacant TWA jet for their flight back home to the United States. Unlike the fresh, naive, and unaware faces of the newly arriving soldiers, however, these men seemed far older and more mature than their years—transformed and forever changed by their 365 days in Vietnam. Once-youthful teenagers had become battle-scarred veterans. They showed deference and respect to the nurses, but several in the group mercilessly taunted the apprehensive male soldiers, castigating them as FNGs (fucking new guys) along with several other choice epithets.

Once inside the relative sanctuary of the Long Binh terminal, Sharon, Kathi, and Rose were ordered to report to the 90th Replacement Battalion the following day for a personal interview with the chief nurse and to receive their Vietnam hospital assignments. Then, they were assigned their overnight quarters in an old house trailer, which had been gutted except for several military cots set up barracks-style for sleeping.

Temporarily free from any responsibilities, Sharon and the other women were finally able to look around the Long Binh area. The city was almost entirely an American creation, a massive military stronghold located some 20 miles north of Saigon. Over 50,000 U.S. troops were stationed in the immediate vicinity. and it was the home of the II Field Force, the III ARVN Corps, as well as the command center for the entire U.S. Army. The 44th Medical Brigade headquarters were likewise located in Long Binh as were three of its hospitals—the 24th, 93rd Evacuation, 74th Field. These substantial military facilities had made Long Binh a primary objective during the previous year's Tet Offensive, but the city's strong defenses successfully withheld the onslaught of enemy troops.

The Vietnamese city of Bien Hoa had been virtually incorporated into the overall Long Binh area. It was here some ten years earlier that Major Dale Buis had been killed by communist guerrillas while serving as a military adviser to the South Vietnamese army. He was the first American casualty in what was destined to become the nation's longest war and whose end was still nowhere in sight when Sharon arrived.

Totally exhausted from their arduous trip across the Pacific Ocean, Sharon and the other nurses looked forward only to a shower, a change of clothes, and a good night's sleep. Shortly after sunset, the enemy began heavy shelling of Long Binh with mortars and rockets. The explosions and return fire came at regular, disturbing intervals throughout the night, but mercifully they were never too close to the trailer. Sharon wrote home later of the experience, "It was real odd down at Long Binh, where we first arrived, it was quiet all day until dark. Then the shelling started and went on until about 5 AM. It is so we can't tell where they are shooting from, I guess." It certainly made for a memorable, albeit sleepless, first night in Vietnam.

Early the next morning, Sharon and her friends reported to the nurse's replacement center. Kathi, a U.S. Army captain, was assigned to the 29th Evacuation Hospital at Can Tho, a facility well to the south located in the Mekong River delta. Rose was ordered to a fully mobile tent hospital at Phu Bai, which was reportedly under constant enemy fire. Sharon was ordered north to Chu Lai and the 312th Evacuation Hospital. The North Carolina reserve unit had been in-country for more than six months, and most of its medical staff was scheduled for rest and recreation rotation. It was imperative to bring in fully qualified nursing replacements to temporarily relieve the personnel. Likewise, preparations were already underway to begin turning over hospital operations gradually to the 91st Evacuation Hospital, which was slated to replace the 312th sometime later that summer. The newly assigned nurses would undoubtedly facilitate a smooth transition.

Having received their duty assignments, the three women spent one more uneventful evening together before shipping out the following day. Both Sharon and Rose were scheduled to fly together to Da Nang and, from there, to their individual hospitals. They returned to the Long Binh airport at 0400 hours, Monday, April

28, to await standby space on a northbound military transport. Several long, boring hours passed before they were able to secure a flight. They were joined onboard by a 28-year old Army warrant officer, Fred Walters. He was a friendly, congenial man who provided good company during the long, slow flight to Da Nang. No one aboard could anticipate that he was destined to be killed just three weeks later on May 22nd when enemy forces shot down the helicopter he was piloting.

Da Nang, the second largest city in South Vietnam, was the very heart of the American war effort in the I-Corps region. Thousands of support and supply troops were stationed there to aid and assist in military operations aimed at protecting the integrity of the 17th parallel and interdicting the constant flow of communist troops infiltrating from the north. Seeing the scope of the urban sprawl below and the enormous amount of military activity, Sharon found it hard to imagine that it had been just four short years since the U.S. Marines had first landed on these very beaches.

The military had moved swiftly to expand and enlarge the city's excellent port and harbor facilities in the horseshoe-shaped Da Nang bay. These facilities were now busy accommodating colossal, ocean-going ships and tankers, each conveying enormous amounts of equipment and supplies to feed the American war machine. Just offshore, U.S. destroyers, frigates, and an occasional battleship prowled the coastal waters.

The Da Nang airbase, notable for its long runways, was home to the 11th Tactical Air Wing. Long-range bombers, filled to capacity with powerful explosives, shared the crowded runways with commercial and military transports. In 1967, the base had been heavily mortared by the Viet Cong in a bold and daring assault. They succeeded in destroying some $75 million dollars worth of aircraft before finally being repulsed. Similarly, during the Tet Offensive, all of Da Nang's military facilities were heavily involved in the intense fighting. By contrast, to the south of the city was the majestic China Beach, a serene in-country R&R center for American GIs located along the banks of the South China Sea. The Red Cross operated a popular recreation center there as well as one farther down the coast at Freedom Hill. The 95th Evacuation Hospital was also located in the immediate vicinity.

First known in the western world as Tourane, Da Nang's urban population had swelled to over 450,000 during the war. Most of the new inhabitants were poor peasant refugees from the adjacent provinces who had been forced to flee from their hamlets and villages because of heavy fighting in the region. The big city did provide some degree of sanctuary, but most of its inhabitants were reduced to a life of menial labor, working for the Americans or the Republican government. Others openly operated within the confines of Da Nang's thriving black market or engaged in prostitution. Most were living in poverty and squalor.

Despite the war, Da Nang remained a mystical and cherished city to the Vietnamese. The Hon River ran through its center, while a narrow isthmus linked the mainland to Monkey Mountain and the small port of Tien Sa. There were several sacred Buddhists pagodas and shrines within the city limits. Just seven miles to the south were the sacred peaks of the Marble Mountains (*Ngu Hanh Son*), which suddenly jutted skyward as a geological wonder. Symbolically representing the traditional five elements of the universe (water, wood, gold, earth, fire), the mountains were honeycombed with caves, Buddhists shrines, and Viet Cong.

When Sharon's plane finally set down in this exotic Asian city, she was surprised by the desolation in the immediate vicinity of the airport. Just the previous day, a work crew had been detailed to burn an enormous pile of garbage, but they were oblivious to the potentially dangerous high winds swirling in the vicinity. A hot cinder from the flames was blown some 800 yards into an ammunition dump full of ordnance. The detonation resulted in a gigantic explosion. The sheer force of the blast destroyed dozens of nearby peasant shacks, killed two people, and injured an additional 200. The resulting fire raged uncontrolled in and around the base for 14 hours despite the best efforts of military firefighters. The ashes were still hot and smoldering when Sharon's plane arrived in the city.

Since there were no southbound planes to Chu Lai scheduled for the remainder of the day and travel at night was deemed too dangerous, Sharon was forced to stay overnight in Da Nang before departing the next day. After almost a week of continuous travel together, she and Rose finally were forced to part company; Rose was scheduled to head north to the hospital at Phu Bai.

Sharon's flight the next day down the coast was mercifully short. She finally arrived at the Ky Ha Airbase in the early afternoon. A U.S. Army jeep was waiting to drive her the remaining two miles to the 312th Evacuation Hospital where she finally reported. After a brief welcome and quick orientation, Sharon was sent to the hospital's supply office where she was issued her new, comfortable fatigues—the standard uniform for all nurses in combat areas in Vietnam. She also received her helmet and an ill-fitting pair of boots. Curiously, the supply office was currently out of flak vests but promised to issue her one as soon as they became available.

Sharon was scheduled to begin formal processing the following day. Her first assignment would be a six-hour nursing shift in the hospital's surgical ward to help her adjust to the time difference and recover from the long days of travel. She was also issued a room on the second floor of what had become informally designated as the "male" BOQ, although there were several other women living there because of space limitations. Unfortunately, her room faced toward the hospital compound, overlooking the volleyball court and the opposite "Chu Lai Hilton," rather than the preferred scenic view of the South China Sea.

Once settled in, Sharon was at last able to change out of her stateside cord uniform and relax. At 2100 hours, she sat down to write her first letter home from Vietnam. She began, *"Finally* arrived at my unit. I never thought it would take so long to get here." Sharon then wrote about the specifics of her trip and everything that had transpired since she had left Canton. "You wouldn't believe all the planes, jeeps, ambulances, and stuff we were in getting up here," she subsequently wrote. "Everything but a helicopter because nurses aren't allowed up in those because of the two who were killed when one crashed."

She described her living quarters in detail including the fact that she was sharing the space with a friendly lizard and several less

The bunker in front of Sharon's quarters at the 312th Evacuation Hospital. She wrote, "Down in front of the building is the bunker. If a siren goes off you have to put on boots, helmet . . . flak jacket and go out to the bunker. The "Chu Lai Hilton" is visible in the background.

amicable mosquitoes, "[My room] is about 8 × 10 feet. The walls are plain, unpainted plywood on three sides. The 4th wall is screen. The ceiling and floor are also plywood. There is a ceiling light and fan—one of those with big wooden paddles. We have to go to supply and get a can of paint and a brush and can paint it however we want. Supply doesn't have any paint at present though . . . Down in front of the building is the bunker. If a siren goes off you have to put on boots, helmet, this heavy vest called a 'flak jacket' (supply is out of those, too) and go out to the bunker.

"Everyone says that this hospital is in the best area of any other hospital in Vietnam. It was just built in [1968] and most of the personnel here came then, as a unit, from Fort Benning, Georgia. Therefore they will all be leaving in August and are now taking their leave time and R & R's. So for the next three weeks or so I'm supposed to work all over to replace those on leave. After that I'll get assigned to a permanent ward."

By now, it was late in the evening and Sharon needed to get some rest. The following day would be the beginning of a rigorous schedule of six-day weeks and long work hours. It was 99 days into the new Nixon administration, the war was still at its peak, hundreds of American boys were being killed and wounded each week. Still, there was some room for optimism. The Paris peace talks had finally progressed beyond the absurd stalemate concerning the shape of the negotiating table, and a substantive breakthrough was always a possibility. Those things were still in other people's hands but all that was really important at this minute to Sharon was to sleep.

7

12 Hour Shifts—6 Days a Week

"I really feel far, far away . . ."

—Letter from Sharon Lane (May 5, 1969)

The month of May, traditionally the first harbinger of summer, was a dangerous time to have arrived in Chu Lai. Despite its scenic beauty and extrinsically serene exterior, tensions were currently running high on the military compound. Recently captured enemy documents strongly suggested that the veteran 3d Regiment, 2d North Vietnamese Army Division, was preparing to launch a series of attacks throughout the I-Corps region, specifically targeting American firebases and large military installations. Rumors were running rampant at the 312th Evacuation Hospital with unsubstantiated stories circulating of impending suicide charges by explosive-laden Viet Cong soldiers and sabotage by the local villagers. Amy Lazar, a Red Cross social worker assigned to the hospital, recorded in her personal log, "You wonder if you will ever be prepared, if you can take the fear that hits your stomach, the sleepless nights waiting for the next attack. There are dozens of rumors that fly around—what is true and what isn't?"

Throughout Chu Lai, everyone remained on a high state of alert. Military intelligence from the Americal Division Headquarters predicted that a major increase in enemy activity in the region would be carefully orchestrated to coincide with the 79th birthday (May 19) of the North Vietnamese president, Ho Chi Minh. In one of her early letters home, Sharon confided, "They are expecting a big offensive from the Viet Cong anytime this month. If it doesn't come, they say it is proof that the VC are losing strength. So [I] have my 'flak' vest and helmet and boots ready every night just in case."

In an effort aimed at preempting the enemy's plans and taking full advantage of the region's dry season, the Americal Division initiated its own offensive in early May of 1969. Using search and destroy tactics along with ongoing ambush patrols, the U.S. Army reported initial success with over 400 Communist troops killed in the immediate vicinity during just the first two weeks of the month. Likewise, a large cache of supplies and weapons were captured which included: ". . . 48 individual weapons, one 122-mm rocket, 126 rounds of RR (Recoilless Rifle) ammunition, 44 RPG (Rocket-Propelled Grenades) rounds, 1,723 Chicom hand-grenades, and assorted explosives." In response, NVA and VC troops launched 159 rockets against U.S. bases throughout Vietnam during a 48-hour time period.

For Lieutenant Lane, the transition to combat nursing was brief. She was initially detailed to work on the hospital's surgical intensive care unit , mercifully one of the few air-conditioned portions of the compound. Unlike her previous duties at Fitzsimons Hospital where she had cared primarily for retired senior officers and elderly coronary patients, Sharon found herself responsible for dozens of young men, all of whom were in their prime of life but now seriously wounded and facing potential death in a distant, foreign land. It was an enormous responsibility but Sharon quickly felt both needed and welcomed at the 312th Evacuation Hospital. "Would you believe I like it here better than at Fitz?" Sharon wrote to her family. "Here everyone needs all the help and friends he can get, so it is much more warm and open."

The 312th surgeons were operating almost continually during this period. Dr. Michael Carey, one of the unit's two neurosurgeons, determined that his 378th Medical Detachment (KE) performed over 330 operations for brain wounds with an additional 70 or so involving spinal cord wounds in just 12 months. All told, his detachment performed as many operations as did the busiest neurosurgical units in northwest Europe during World War II. But this amount of medical activity was characteristic of the 312th as a whole and, indeed, all American hospitals in Vietnam. Unlike their World War II counterparts which were often closed for extended periods of time as they moved from one area to another, the evacuation hospitals in Vietnam were always open, receiving casualties day-after-day. Such work without respite proved particularly hard on the nursing staff who continued to work on the wards even when there was a lull in the fighting while the doctors rested.

The American Red Cross was also active in Vietnam. Part of its mission was to assist doctors and nurses at Army hospitals with social workers serving as the primary liaison between a wounded GI and his family. Shortly after admission to the hospital, a health and welfare report was frequently compiled on an injured soldier. Its purpose was to help reassure the GI's family and provide some substantive information about the scope and nature of the injuries that he had sustained. For those grievously injured patients who were either unconscious or unable to speak, a doctor's interpretative statement was taken instead and wired back to the United States by the Red Cross. It contained an explanation of the soldier's current medical condition and his overall prognosis.

During the 1969 spring offensive, Amy Lazar filled out dozens of such documents while she was with the 312th Evacuation Hospital. In the personal log, she wrote about the influx of casualties, "[We] have had some fairly serious casualties recently including a bilateral amputee, several head cases, and about eleven GI's on the serious or very seriously ill list . . . we still continue to accept numerous casualties from the LZs (landing zones). Raids through the perimeters have been numerous at Bandy, Gator, etc. Fighting is very heavy out in the field . . . [as] casualties continue to pour

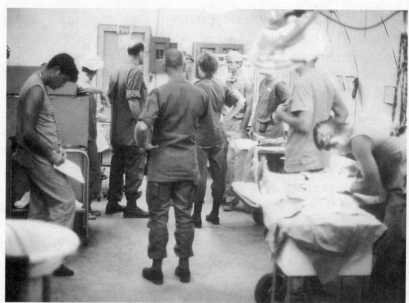

Doctors and nurses in the preop area at the 312th. Minor surgery was often performed here. The hospital treated over 10,000 patients in its first 8 months in Vietnam and had a remarkable 98 percent save rate.

DR. MICHAEL CAREY

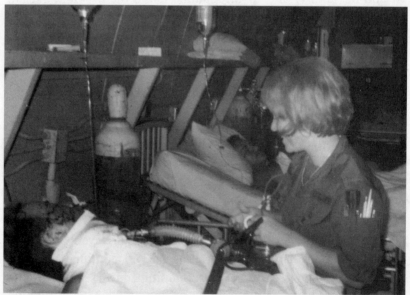

A 312th nurse checks on a seriously injured GI. The average age of nurses in Vietnam was just 23.

MARY SMITH

in." Sharon independently confirmed the intensity of the spring fighting in her own personal correspondence, "The hospital is equipped to handle 250 patients. We had 250 plus we were getting in 50 a day and sending out 50 a day. [We] have really been getting the patients though—both GIs and Vietnamese . . . Surgery has been going on *continuously* for 3 days and nights. One doctor has gotten 6 hours sleep in 3 days. The offensive is really on."

After a casualty had been admitted and undergone surgery, he was sent to the intensive care ward for observation and recovery. There, the surgeon or treating physician would continue to follow each patient and regularly check on his progress. A complete list of explicit medical instructions was given to the nurses and could easily run several pages depending upon the severity of a patient's wounds. They would detail the types and doses of medications to be administered, the rate of intravenous drips, a schedule for checking and changing bandages, and other important orders. With as many as 25 patients assigned to the ward at any given time, the 312th nurses and corpsmen were constantly busy during their 12-hour shifts monitoring blood pressure, draining chest and gastric tubes, accurately charting their patients' physical condition, and tending to their many needs.

In the event of an unexpected emergency when a physician was not immediately available, the nurses were expected to assume the primary responsibility for performing lifesaving measures, relying on their own professional medical judgment. Lieutenant Mary Mentzger recalled that during one late night shift on the intensive care ward, she discovered during her routine rounds that a recently admitted patient had bled out after surgery. His bed sheets were soaked with blood and entering the early stages of agonal breathing, a positive indication that death was imminent. There was no time to summon the on-duty doctor to the ward, so Mentzger ordered an immediate transfusion of two units of blood and initiated other medical procedures that were responsible for saving the soldier's life. The doctors, in fact, absolutely came to depend on the nurses' and corpsmen's ability and judgment at the hospital; both groups were accorded a great deal of respect. A team atmosphere prevailed on the compound. Several of the doctors took the time, when circumstances allowed, to explain and demonstrate advanced medical concepts and surgical techniques to the nurses.

Despite the overwhelming challenges of wartime medicine, the nurses (whose average age was just 23 years) were forced to personally confront the sober realities of their own mortality. Even though the 312th Evacuation Hospital had a remarkable 98 percent save rate, the fragility of life was painfully apparent in the reality of gaping chest wounds, traumatic amputations, brain wounds, and patients gradually suffocating to death over several days from the so-called "wet lung syndrome." Sharon, in a letter home, wrote to her parents about what amounted to a fairly routine day at the hospital: "A GI with malaria died. Another with multiple gunshot and fragment wounds was bad all day but still [is] living. I gave him nine units of blood and two of units of plasma. He has a leaking artery graft in his left leg. [The] bleeding has finally slowed down but [there is] not enough circulation to the leg and foot. [He] probably will have to have it amputated yet . . . We had a little Vietnamese girl start bleeding from her colostomy at 7 PM a couple of nights ago. I came back to work in the morning at 7 AM and she was still bleeding and had gotten three units of blood. She kept bleeding until noon and they finally took her back into surgery with a blood pressure of 84/ and she was partially in shock. I took care of her today in ICU and she looks pretty good and will probably go back to the [Vietnamese] ward tomorrow."

The flood of casualties continued to arrive at the hospital through mid-May; most came from battles without names and from a war whose progress could be neither illustrated nor charted on maps. The American wounded universally held the nurses at the hospital in high esteem, since in many respects the women represented the life that the men had left behind in the United States.

The primary mission of the 312th Evacuation Hospital was to stabilize the wounded and prepare them for rapid air-evacuation. The entire process was designed to be quick and efficient, usually taking no more than a week. Thus, the ultimate fate of many of the soldiers, which the medical staff had labored so hard to save, remained forever a mystery to them. However, there always seemed to be an exception. For Sharon and many of the other nurses, it was a 23-year-old private, who had been assigned to the 502nd Infantry, 101st Airborne Division (the Screaming Eagles), and was involved in the early fighting for a mountain that the military designated merely as Hill #937. To the soldiers involved in the brutal struggle for its ridges, however, it became more appropriately known as "Hamburger Hill." Located in the A Shau Valley along one of the NVA's primary infiltration routes into the south, the developing battle proved atypical for Vietnam since it involved large concentrations of forces on both sides locked in a protracted engagement.

On May 7, the young private received a serious abdominal wound and was medevaced to the 27th Surgical Hospital in Chu Lai, a medical facility located just to the southwest of the U.S. Marine Airfield and about three miles away from the 312th Evacuation Hospital. There, after being X-rayed, he was taken into surgery where it was discovered that the bullet had nicked his bowel, greatly increasing the potential risk of infection. Still, the overall prognosis remained good and the attending doctors at the 27th Surgical anticipated that their patient would make a full and complete recovery. Indeed, it appeared that he had received the coveted "million-dollar wound," one that was not life-threatening but serious enough to necessitate a return to the United States to convalesce.

After just a few days at the surgical hospital, the soldier was transferred to the 312th Evacuation Hospital for some additional postoperative treatment and to be readied for air-evacuation to Japan. On the eve of his scheduled departure, one of the hospital surgeons discovered evidence of a serious bacterial infection. Additional surgery was immediately ordered. It confirmed that he had developed peritonitis. Now far too ill to be moved, he was placed under continuous care in the ICU where Sharon Lane, Mary Mentzger, and several of the other 312th Evacuation Hospital's nursing staff cared for him. All the staff found him to be an ideal patient as well as a pleasant, articulate, and intelligent young man. They learned that he had married his high school sweetheart and, while in college, the young couple both worked jobs to earn enough money so that he could complete his education. Just after receiving his degree, he lost his draft deferment, was reclassified 1-A by the local Selective Service Board, and promptly received an induction notice. A short time later, after completing basic training, he was ordered to Vietnam.

The young soldier became increasingly fatalistic after undergoing a second surgery. The massive doses of intravenous antibiotics seemed to have little effect in controlling his raging infection, and his weight plummeted to just 85 pounds. The hospital's doctors were both frustrated and helpless as they watched their patient develop gangrene, stress ulcers, and virtually every other medical complication imaginable. Finally, they ordered the private evacuated to Yokohama, Japan, where his young wife arrived at his bedside just two hours before he died.

Throughout the 312th Evacuation Hospital, this fatality was mourned more than most others; however, grief was a luxury that a busy hospital could ill afford. With more incoming wounded always on the way, duty necessarily took precedence over personal emotions. For everyone, it seemed as if the world outside Vietnam and the Chu Lai compound had all but ceased to exist—work had become the only reality. Each day—each shift—was all that ultimately mattered. Despite her short time with the unit, Sharon quickly became an integral part of the 312th Evacuation Hospital and was a seasoned veteran. She seemed to be doing something important with her life and was content.

Everyday life in the hospital compound would have been considered difficult by contemporary American standards. It was still seen as excellent duty by those fortunate enough to be stationed at Chu Lai and was, in reality, a relatively safe assignment; but Sharon quickly found that she missed many of the amenities and conveniences of stateside life. Her quarters on the second floor of the male BOQ meant that each time she wished to use the restroom or shower

An aerial view of the 312th Evacuation Hospital complex looking northward. The BOQ's and the Officer's Club are located on the point to the extreme right while the medical wards and the amphitheater are visible in the background.

Two Vietnamese civilian workers walk down the street between the doctors' "hooches" (left) and the 312th hospital complex (right). The doctors were located near the hospital in order to be quickly available to handle emergencies.

facilities, she was forced to walk outside and across the volleyball court, which was usually in use between of 1600 and 1800 hours. This inconvenience was made even more complicated because she had neglected to bring her bathrobe. "Every time I get over to the washroom," Sharon wrote on May 1, "I find out that [have] forgotten something—razor, soap, comb, toothpaste, or something." Still, the searing sun ensured a constant supply of hot water for showers even though there were no stalls for privacy. Flush toilets were a recent addition, but despite this luxury, the pungent smell from the latrines still permeated the compound on occasion. The base's water supply was treated with iodine for medicinal and purification purposes. After washing in this treated water, everyone's towels and light-colored clothing turned orange including her favorite pair of white, off-duty Levis, to Sharon's dismay.

After a few days with the hospital, Sharon finally found time to go down to the supply depot to get some paint for the door to her quarters. She discovered they were typically out of stock. She wrote, "We have to go to supply and get a can of paint and a brush and we can paint [our rooms] however we want. Supply doesn't have any paint at present though." When it did finally arrive, the color choices were so limited that Sharon was forced to settle for a gallon of green paint, which she used during her off-duty hours to paint the walls of her room and a chest of drawers. After that was depleted, she obtained a can of black paint, which she used on the floor and the façade of her door, a color choice that many of the doctors and nurses quietly found curious and somewhat morbid.

The food at the hospital proved to be surprisingly palatable and plentiful. Each week, the mess hall cooks served a good variety of steak, pizza, shrimp, baked potatoes, and other American-style dishes. Sharon did miss some of her favorite foods, such as yogurt, potato chips, and soda pop, but there was always the Officer's Club where such fare (except for the yogurt) was available. Still, she wrote home, "The food has been real good. Tonight we had Chop Suey which was very good. For lunch we had hamburgers with home-made buns. The milk is all of the 'powdered' variety. The ice-cream has been pineapple every day so far. Ugh . . . We can go to the mess hall only at specific hours and, otherwise, there is no place to get food . . . You don't know how nice it is to be able to get something to eat whenever you want it. Over here, there is nothing except water after mealtime . . . [Still] I have been eating like a horse and am still hungry all of the time. You must really burn up the calories over here. I have never eaten this much before."

After finishing her long nursing shift, Sharon usually went back to her quarters after supper to relax and write letters. Early on, she made friends with a doctor from San Francisco who headed up the hospital's laboratory. He would often stop by to talk and visit with Sharon. He graciously loaned her his personal radio since the Chu Lai exchange had none available, and she had become accustomed to sleeping with music playing. She wrote, "[I] am going to buy a radio some time . . . The reception here is good—surprisingly. The PX sells them as fast as the get them in . . . [I] have had Jim's in my room for a week. Keep telling him to take it back [since] he never gets to listen to it . . . [We] get state-side type music from Radio Saigon [and] listen to Hanoi Hanna some nights. She is always saying, We haven't forgotten you Americans in Chu Lai. You have 'one more week to live' . . . and stuff like that. We just laugh."

Sharon occasionally went to one of the nightly movies shown in the courtyard located just outside the mess hall on a large, painted plywood screen. One evening, she and a group of friends watched from the building's roof the popular thriller, *Grand Slam*, starring Janet Leigh and Edward G. Robinson. Afterwards, they successfully fooled the mess hall chief into believing they were all celebrating one nurse's birthday. He defied regulations and allowed the group into the kitchen where they prepared two homemade pizzas loaded full of salami, hamburger, cheese, and mushrooms.

The Officer's Club was another popular diversion, although Sharon found it far too cold to spend much time there. "I rarely go over [to the club]. It is air-conditioned with a stolen air-conditioner from a dock at Da Nang. A couple of enlisted men stole it a couple of months ago. It is supposed to be for an airplane hangar so you can imaging how cold it makes the club. I just can't stand it."

The club had regular entertainment there and even live music performed by a band wholly comprised of hospital staff. Each night, it was a popular diversion to sit and watch from the club's balcony as the Huey flare-ships dropped their cargoes in a beautiful, pyrotechnic display, covering the countryside in an eerie dirty orange glow and black silhouettes. Regular, well-attended lectures, were also held in an ongoing effort to keep everyone informed about the progress of the war. In early May, a colonel from the Americal Division was invited to explain the regional pacification program being conducted in the Chu Lai area. This program optimistically included a plan for eliminating the entire Viet Cong infrastructure and establishing a local democratic government. The military also hoped to construct a sugar mill to stimulate industry and provide jobs for the surrounding peasants. At the same time, humanitarian Medical Civil Action Patrols (MEDCAPs) programs were being conducted at the nearby villages of An Ton and Samhi.

Lieutenant Leta Menton recalled an even more dramatic presentation which featured a Viet Cong soldier dressed in stereotypical black pajamas. Through an interpreter, he described the nature of the war from the North's perspective and explained that the Americans were seen by most of the Vietnamese as invaders who had merely replaced the imperialistic French. Communism as a Marxist/Leninist ideology meant little to the average soldier. The Viet Cong believed that the war was being fought primarily for nationalistic motives. If the Americans were not in Vietnam, he concluded, there would be no war. This sober assessment of the war effort was a shock to everyone in attendance. It was the first time they realized that, to many Vietnamese, the United States was not welcome in their country.

Sharon and the other nurses put in long hours and were entitled only to one day off per week. "I am working 12-hours a day so I don't have much spare time," Sharon wrote. "I get one day off a week and usually spend it washing clothes and cleaning my room." On May 13, Sharon decided to go to the exchange located about a quarter-mile outside of the entrance to the hospital compound to buy some shampoo. There, she met a friendly GI named Frank from Puerto Rico. He was temporarily in from the field. The two walked the short distance down to the beach where they spent the rest of the day relaxing and enjoying each other's company. Sharon wrote, "I started talking to one of the soldiers [at the PX] and went down to the USO club with him. We stayed there all day. There are about three or four wooden buildings where the guys go to relax. There is a pool table, three Ping-Pong tables, card tables, a reading room, and such there. We played four games of checkers, crazy 8's, and 500 rummy. And he taught me a card game, but I don't remember what the name of it was. That was the first time I've been away from the hospital area. He was quite a character, an infantryman out in the field."

Sharon went to the beach on one other occasion to sunbathe and swim. She wrote, "Went swimming last Monday. It is really hard to get down to the beach though. Have to climb down the cliff. Slid down part way that day and scrapped up my left elbow and got my 'seat' all dirty. They have dug out steps a couple of times, I guess, but when it rains they wash away. It is about a straight up and down path. We are only allowed to swim in two places. The rest of the beach is off limits due to possible 'mines.' The water is real rough and there is a swift under-current so all I did was wade around. There have been a few guys disappear over by the USO club swim area and they are thought to have drowned [after having been carried off by the undertow]. The water is pretty warm and salty." After laying out for just two hours in the hot sun, Sharon paid with a painful sunburn.

The inviting beaches and picturesque waters of the South China Sea seemed to be ideal for water sports. Several of the doctors at the hospital built an entire boat from scratch while another enterprising physician began a letter-writing campaign to various California boat manufacturers requesting that they donate a sailboat to the hospital. He argued that sailing in the placid seas off-shore would have a therapeutic value for the doctors and staff. Miraculously, a 21-foot sailboat equipped with a 3-foot keel was somehow delivered from the United States to the hospital. The military was neither enthusiastic nor pleased about this event. Indeed, it was feared that a boat in full sail would pose an inviting target for enemy snipers, so permission to launch the vessel was denied. The sailboat remained dry-docked and immobile resting on wooden supports in front of the 312th's dental clinic at the very west end of the hospital and facing inland towards the mountains.

The closest Vietnamese settlement to the hospital was the village of An Ton. Located just two miles to the west, the small hamlet was situated along Highway 1, the country's main thoroughfare, next to the Song An Ton River. Nearby, thousands of displaced people were housed in primitive, makeshift shelters constructed from packing crates, plywood, and other cast-off materials scavenged from military trash dumps. Most of these refugees had fled to the Chu Lai area because of the years of intense fighting in the region.

Virtually all the Vietnamese in An Ton earned their living by catering to the appetites of the Americans. While the village was off-limits to Sharon and the other nurses, GIs from the surrounding bases were regular customers of the prostitutes who conducted business openly nearby. Consequently, the hospital's medical ward was kept busy treating numerous cases of venereal disease. Also, a thriving black market sold illicit alcohol, cigarettes, and other contraband articles; even marijuana was readily available. In fact, drug usage among soldiers had already begun to pose a problem during the late 1960s for American military commanders. A contemporary report from the Americal Division Headquarters warned, "Racial incidents and disturbances have become an serious and explosive problem. Most instances occur late in the evening or shortly after midnight. Investigators reveal that marijuana or alcohol are almost always involved to some degree . . . Extremely loose control measures over personnel in stand down status is obvious throughout Chu Lai installation and brigade base camp."

The most coveted and respectable work for the Vietnamese civilian population was on the American base camps themselves. Those fortunate enough to obtain a work permit assisted the military in a variety of tasks. Some Vietnamese women at the hospital were assigned to the wards and helped the nurses tend to their patients. The vast majority, however, worked as simple domestics or, as they were popularly known, as hootch maids or *mamma-sans*. They cleaned the doctors and nurses' quarters, laundered their fatigues, polished their boots, and completed a variety of other domestic chores for just $10 per month.

The wealth of the Americans was overwhelming to these impoverished people, and they would often pilfer small items while working. Sharon, who was fairly petite, found that she was particularly vulnerable: "You can have [your *mamma-san*] launder your clothes but they say you only get half of them back—especially if you wear small sizes. She keeps whatever she likes. So I have my bathing suit and some other stuff locked in my duffel bag. I am glad I brought the lock."

It was commonly believed that the Vietnamese civilians who worked on the base camps were informants for the Viet Cong. Indeed, there was a strong correlation between high absenteeism and enemy attacks. "No *mamma-san* today. Guess they have some kind of holiday," Sharon wrote. "Thought maybe we'd be hit today when the *mamma-sans* didn't come in from the village but found out they had a holiday. Usually they get wind of impending attacks and don't come in on those days. Everyone was on the alert for nothing this time . . . Some are suspected to be either VC or VC supporters."

Military alerts at the 312th Evacuation Hospital had become fairly common in May with the overall increase in military activity in the I-Corps theater. A gray alert was meant to warn the staff that there was a potential for enemy incoming fire. Base personnel were expected to take appropriate precautions that usually entailed wearing flak vests and helmets as well as being prepared to seek refuge in one of the hospital's many bunkers. Yellow alerts increased the base's readiness further while a red alert was sounded by siren when the hospital was actually under attack. Unlike mortar fire, which provided some advanced warning before impact, the rockets used against the 312th Evacuation Hospital were preceded by only a momentary swishing sound and then followed by a terrific explosion almost immediately. Most of the time, when the alert sirens finally sounded, the enemy attack was already over and the damage was done.

Complicating the situation were many false alarms. On one occasion, the battleship *USS New Jersey* shelled the coast with its powerful 16-inch guns. Although the shells were aimed inland, the unexpected bombardment sent the entire hospital scrambling for cover. Exploding ordnance, air strikes, and friendly fire were likewise often misconstrued as an enemy attack. On May 12, at 0245 hours, an alert was sounded; all the off-duty hospital personnel quickly sought cover under their beds or in sandbagged bunkers. The nurses working the night shift, oblivious to their own safety, first tended to their patients. They covered the nonambulatory ones with mattresses for protection against shrapnel and saw to it that the others were safely under their beds. After about 20 minutes, the all clear sounded and everyone returned to their quarters, bemoaning their lost sleep and the inconvenience.

With the onset of daylight later that morning, the danger of attack was greatly diminished since any enemy rocket launches could be easily detected by American military spotters. To everyone's surprise at 1000 hours, two Soviet built 122-mm rockets slammed into the hospital compound. One did not detonate and its warhead was imbedded in the soil while the other scored a direct hit on the 21-foot parked next to the dental clinic. The hospital dentist at work in the clinic received a minor wound but nobody was seriously injured although the boat, which absorbed the total force of the rocket's impact, was totally demolished. Amy Lazar wrote, "We got hit again. Broad daylight—imagine that!! This time they landed another on our compound right in front of the dental clinic. Fortunately no one was near at the time and it made a direct hit on the $5,000 sailboat sitting out front." Sharon, who was on duty at the time, also wrote, ". . . a rocket hit a beached [sailboat] and blew it into a million pieces. The dental clinic was closest to it and a dentist got slightly hurt. I was at work at the time . . . and was setting up IV's. We got all of the patients under the beds that we could and

DR. MICHAEL CAREY

A 21-foot sailboat in front of the 312th Evacuation Hospital's dental clinic. The boat was delivered to the hospital after an intensive letter writing campaign by one of the hospital's doctors.

DR. MICHAEL CAREY

The remains of the sailboat after taking a direct hit by a 122-mm rocket. The attack was unusual because it occurred during broad daylight.

put mattresses over the ones in traction, etc. Very interesting place but hardly anyone here is scared though. It is just like part of the job." One of the physicians with more experience in Vietnam put it more accurately, "You say more 'Hail Mary's' over here than anytime in your life."

The majority of the 312th Evacuation Hospital's medical staff had been in-country for over six months. These doctors and nurses were slated for R&R leave. When combined with the fact that all the reservists were scheduled to depart Vietnam and return to North Carolina in late August, it meant that a large number of replacement nurses and doctors were immediately needed in Chu Lai. In early May, the 44th Medical Brigade Headquarters ordered the transfer of the entire 91st Evacuation Hospital from its location at Tuy Hoa to help ease the unit's personnel needs and gradually assume the overall operations of the 312th hospital at Chu Lai. According to military records, the 91st Evacuation Hospital was no longer needed down south since "[Its] patient census, particularly with respect to U.S. patients, [is] low and maintenance of the hospital plant at an acceptable level was difficult. The hospital [is presently] located in an isolated environment and [is] experiencing problems in such areas as security, maintenance, and logistical support."

For Sharon and the other replacement staff slated to remain on after the 312th Evacuation Hospital had departed, the news of an impending change of command was not particularly welcomed. The 91st was a regular army unit, having been established in 1918 during the first World War. It was universally feared that the low-key atmosphere prevailing at the hospital would soon disappear. Sharon wrote privately after the arrival of the first 91st Evacuation Hospital's nurses, "They are from the unit who will take over when the 312th goes home in September. Their hospital is further south somewhere. They are handling 80% Vietnamese casualties now and are turning their hospital over to the Viets and coming here to take over. We are supposed to get the new chief nurse tomorrow. So the

unit will change names in September . . . however, they are supposed to be a RA (regular Army) group—not a reserve unit like the
312th is. Things are supposed to get a lot more 'strict Army style.'
No one is looking forward to it." At that time, though, the only
obvious change was cosmetic: the hospital was referred to jointly as
the 312th/91st Evacuation Hospital.

After first working on the surgical intensive care unit, Sharon
was permanently transferred to Ward 4, the Vietnamese section of
the hospital, although she continued to spend one day a week in
intensive care. Ward 4 of the hospital was inevitably shorthanded
and overworked as Sharon quickly discovered, "We work really
hard. Actually we never get done on our ward since we are continuously getting patients in, cleaning them up, and sending them on
to Vietnamese hospitals." The head nurse kept a sign behind the
nurse's station that reminded everyone to "love thy Vietnamese,"
which was left open to interpretation.

The language barrier was the most difficult obstacle for the nurses
to overcome and a constant source of frustration. Even the few
rudimentary Vietnamese phrases they were able to master were of
little or no help. A Vietnamese translator was regularly available
during the daylight shift, but overall communication with the patients remained poor. This situation was further complicated by the
Vietnamese's natural intimidation at being sick or wounded in a
strange, foreign hospital.

The patients were of varying ages, from mere infants to the elderly and infirm. Because of space and staff limitations, there was
no isolation policy nor any privacy. Women and children were
housed together; surgical patients intermingled with medical cases,
despite the potential for cross-contamination. Many of the patients
were in need of constant monitoring because of the severity of their
condition. Also, it seemed that everyone's recuperation was hampered by the incessant heat complicated by the lack of adequate
ventilation on the ward, which was cooled only by open, screened
windows and a few strategically positioned fans. Night hours (1900–
0700) were the preferred shift. A well-known late riser, Sharon was

eagerly anticipating the time when she could volunteer for the night shift.

The condition of the Vietnamese peasants proved to be quite a shock to Sharon. Some of the Montagnards (mountain people) had never seen running water. Virtually all the patients arrived filthy and dirty from the unsanitary conditions prevalent in their villages and hamlets. It took several antiseptic bathings to remove the squalor of poverty. Besides their wounds, injuries, and illnesses, all the Vietnamese patients suffered from a variety of complicating ailments inherent to much of the Third World: severe anemia, intestinal parasites, tuberculosis, and malaria. Sharon wrote home in detail about her work on the Vietnamese ward on May 5: "[I] am now on the least liked ward here—the Vietnamese ward. The census is around 40 and we have five Viet Cong prisoners and three South Vietnamese soldiers while the rest are South Vietnamese civilians. You wouldn't *believe* that ward. There is an MP there all the time to make sure that the prisoners don't escape and that the other patients don't 'do them in.' Some of the patients are medical—TB, malaria, malnutrition, pneumonia, etc. Most of them are surgical though—gunshot wounds and mortar and fragment wounds and burns. The sickest ones have a family member with them who bathes them and feeds them. So we have to feed the families as well as the patients at mealtime.

"These are the dirtiest people I could ever imagine. They *all* have intestinal worms and you can see them in the BM. They all have old, healed (and unhealed) sores and scars all over . . . Two nights ago [I] was taking care of this 11-year-old boy with a gunshot wound of the abdomen . . . Just put a towel over him for a diaper and he had a huge, liquid BM. Took it off and was washing it out in a pan of water and got this thing wrapped around my hand. Was about an eight inch bowel worm. Nearly scared the BM out of me when [I] first saw it. It was dead though. Never moved, anyway. So tossed it in the waste paper can. Am now more cautious when washing out stuff like that. Never know what you will find . . .

"The patients leave our ward after about a week and are sent to province hospitals run by the Vietnamese. None of them want to

DR. MICHAEL CAREY

Two Vietnamese girls after being treated at the 312th Evacuation Hospital. Sharon was stationed in Ward 4 during most of her time with the hospital and often worked with such patients.

go there because the doctors don't know anything about medicine. They go out of here by helicopter. When they get there, the doctors take their IV's out, dressings off and casts off of broken bones . . . One man with a broken leg was sent out and came back to us in two days. They had taken his cast off and the bones got displaced again with one end coming through the skin . . . There are some water pitchers in the supply room and I couldn't figure out why they didn't pass them out because all you get done is getting cups of water for people. The corpsman said though that the [patients] use the pitchers to urinate in . . . so we don't use the pitchers. Good policy . . . Oh, also, this one man had an IV running and he got thirsty so his disconnected the tubing from the needle and was lying there with the tubing in his mouth drinking the IV."

Despite such obstacles, Sharon still enjoyed working on the ward. The Vietnamese children were gentle and loving with the younger, less seriously hurt ones, often sitting on the nurses' laps to cuddle. It was easy for Sharon and the other nurses to love them for they were obviously the innocent and unintended victims of the war. Each day, the nurses set out a bowl of candy to the delight of the children. Although they tried to ration their consumption of the treats to reasonable amounts, many of the children would quietly sneak up the nurses' station to steal a piece when the nurses and corpsmen were preoccupied. The practice itself seemed harmless enough until a serious hepatitis epidemic broke out on the ward. It was later determined that children had inadvertently contaminated the bowl of candy with their dirty hands, thereby transmitting the infection. When wiser heads prevailed, and cellophane-wrapped sweets were substituted for the unwrapped candy and the problem resolved itself.

On May 13, Sharon was told that she was scheduled to begin the night shift on Ward 4 the following day. She celebrated by sleeping late and looking forward to the cool nights and the freedom it promised.

8

Nurses Aren't Supposed to Die

"I have lost a wonderful daughter . . ."

—John Lane quoted by the Tribune Wire Services
(June 11, 1969)

Richard M. Nixon was elected the 37th President of the United States in 1968 on the firm pledge to bring "peace with honor" to Vietnam. He hinted during the campaign of a secret plan to end the war. Initially, the new administration pursued a "fight-and-talk" strategy, hoping to force some progress in the Paris peace negotiations by exerting America's will on the battlefield. The talks were hopelessly stalemated because of the North Vietnamese delegation's intransigence and its insistence that the United States make a complete, unilateral troop withdrawal from Vietnam coupled with the removal of the South Vietnamese President, Nguyen Van Thieu. Such terms were still unacceptable during the winter of 1969.

Early on, President Nixon ordered a comprehensive review of the political and military situation in Southeast Asia to help assist him in formulating a new, effective Vietnamese policy. The reports, however, were discouraging especially with regard to the fighting capabilities of the Army of the Republic of Vietnam (ARVN). Much of the officer corps was corrupt, filled with political appointments, and lacking in effective leadership. The general ranks were plagued by desertions. American troops sarcastically referred to any combat mission in conjunction with ARVN forces as "search and avoid." Indeed, the South Vietnamese had come increasingly to rely on American air and firepower to stave off defeat while U.S. military commanders had been forced to assume a disproportionate responsibility for the fighting.

With domestic unrest within the United States at its peak and the American death toll in Vietnam exceeding 35,000, there was enormous political pressure on President Nixon to take some sort of action that would show tangible signs of progress in the war. On March 5, the Secretary of Defense, Melvin Laird, was dispatched to Saigon by the President as his personal emissary to gather information that would help formulate just such a plan. When Secretary Laird returned to Washington, he urged the President to begin a phased withdrawal of American troops while gradually turning over responsibility for the fighting to the ARVN forces. The United States would continue to provide additional training, support, and airpower during this period while disengaging from its active ground combat role. The policy, known as "Vietnamization," was secretly scheduled to begin by July 1 with the first removal of American troops and continue through 14 steps until all American forces had been totally withdrawn. President Nixon later justified these action in his memoirs, ". . . withdrawing a number of American combat troops from Vietnam would demonstrate to Hanoi that we were serious in seeking a diplomatic settlement; it might also calm domestic public opinion by graphically demonstrating the we were beginning to wind down the war . . . This decision was another turning point in my administration's Vietnam policy." In essence, the United States was slowly returning to its advisory role similar to the one that had existed under both the Eisenhower and Kennedy administrations.

The major obstacle to the new policy initiated by Nixon would undoubtedly be South Vietnamese President Nguyen Van Thieu. He openly feared that the withdrawal of even a small number of

American forces would be interpreted by North Vietnam as a loss of American commitment in Southeast Asia. Likewise, he was convinced that such actions were premature, given the stark battlefield realities of the war. So in early June, President Nixon arranged to hold a summit meeting with his South Vietnamese counterpart on isolated Midway Island. It was to be the first personal meeting between the two heads of state. The hope was that the talks would result in meaningful progress toward bringing the war to a swift and successful conclusion.

After the two week offensive by American forces concluded in early May, there was a brief lull in the fighting throughout much of the I-Corps region. The 312th Evacuation Hospital continued to receive casualties but in quick spurts of activity. Nothing compared to the mass-casualty situations of early May. Still, on June 2, the hospital reached an impressive milestone by treating its 10,000th patient, a feat made even more impressive since the 312th had been in Vietnam for only eight months.

During this time, Sharon was enjoying working the night shift on the Vietnamese ward. For much of the night, Sharon's Vietnamese patients were sedated and sleeping while she and the other nurses on duty conducted their rounds by flashlight, quietly checking vital signs, administering medications through IV's, and monitoring patient status. In the morning after assisting with breakfast, Sharon's relief reported for duty at 0645 hours, leaving her free to go to the mess hall, the exchange, or just to bed. It was admittedly difficult to sleep during the hot daylight hours, especially with the incessant noise from incoming helicopters. It was never really quiet on the compound at any time. Even at night, the roar of jets from the U.S. Marine airbase was a constant interruption, and there were enough alerts to make it difficult to get a truly restful sleep. Regardless, Sharon was very happy since she no longer had to face the prospect of getting up at the ungodly hour of 0530 to get ready to report for work.

President Richard M. Nixon greets South Vietnamese President Nguyen Van Thieu at the Midway Island Conference in June 1969. The President used the meetings to announce the first American troop withdrawals from South Vietnam.

NATIONAL ARCHIVES

On Sunday, June 1, after completing her shift, Sharon went to a church service held at the small, interdenominational chapel located near the center of the hospital compound. Sharon wrote, "[I] went to church yesterday . . . We have a small chapel that seats about 40, at the most. It has an organ. The minister wears his fatigues and we do too. The sermon was about 10 minutes long with the whole service only about a half hour. [I] went one other time, the first Sunday I was here. They are trying to organize a choir and have choir practice every Thursday night. They have been trying since December and so far have three nurses and two men signed up."

On Wednesday, June 4th, she wrote to her parents, "[I] worked in ICU again today. [I] was lucky [since] it got to 102°, and ICU is air-conditioned. They have a lot of really sick patients. Had three die yesterday. They still have four on respirators. None too good, either.

"One of the GIs who died yesterday was from Ward 8, medical. [He] had malaria. During the previous night, he had been nauseated and kept getting up to go to the latrine to vomit. He got up at 2 AM and was running to the latrine. [He] ran into a water cooler which threw him backwards [and] fell really hard and cracked his head on the cement floor. The nurse who was on duty said you could *hear* his skull fracture. He immediately started bleeding from the ears and nose and stopped breathing. Then had cardiac arrest. They got him going again (Dr. Michael Carey trephined the soldier to make sure he did not have an operable blood clot compressing his brain) and transferred him to ICU but he died anyway yesterday. [He] had severe brain damage. [The] other death was a GI with multiple fragment wounds from a mine explosion. He was there two weeks ago when I worked that other day in ICU. Also a Vietnamese died but I don't know what was wrong with him."

The beginning of the Midway Island summit between Nixon and Thieu in June led to an increase in tensions throughout Chu Lai for it was feared that the enemy might attempt to disrupt the meeting with some bold military move. The American Division had recently captured an enemy prisoner who, after interrogation, seemed to give credence to the rumors that were circulating. So on the evening of June 7, many of the doctors and nurses at the 312th Evacuation Hospital reported for their night shifts equipped with flak vests and helmets. Dr. Michael Carey, one of the unit's two neurosurgeons, chose to sleep on the cement floor next to a cement wall in one of the two vacant operating rooms as a precaution. For others, though, it was just another routine evening. The Officer's Club was having yet another "happy hour" with those in attendance celebrating the final performance of the 312th's amateur band. To commemorate this auspicious event, its members passed out souvenir lighters engraved, "Taco, Friz, and Quack—For Many Happy Hours—312th Medical Society."

By early June, Sergeant Rick Castilla and his platoon of 20 men from the 198th Light Infantry Brigade had been out in the bush for several weeks. Their nightly mission was to sweep an assigned sector of about 5,000 square yards and then set up ambush positions, using claymore mines and trip wires along the area's primitive trails. To maximize their effectiveness, Castilla divided his unit into three squads, careful to move each of them a good distance away from one another to lessen the potential of a "friendly fire" incident.

Castilla's troops were just a few miles away from the main Americal Division headquarters in Chu Lai and from the 312th Evacuation Hospital. The terrain, however, was very different from the sandy areas of the coastal plain. They were surrounded by thick vegetation that obscured their vision; the rolling foothills were honeycombed with small paths that served as major enemy infiltration routes. With the sanctuary provided by the darkness, the NVA troops were undoubtedly on the move, secretly entering the surrounding villages to pick up food and supplies, and to pay off informants.

The night of June 7 and the early morning of June 8 were quiet, illuminated only by the dim light of a fading moon. There had been no enemy contact for Castilla's platoon, just the misery of being out in the field, eating C-rations, and waiting for something to happen.

With the first streaks of light on the eastern horizon anticipating dawn, the Americans broke down their positions, packed away their mines, and began to move slowly toward a predetermined rendezvous point. To signal the other parts of his platoon, Sergeant Castilla set off a star-cluster flare to identify his position in the deep savanna brush. Almost immediately, the loud whooshing sound of two rockets being fired was heard, startling the Americans. From a separate location a good distance away, another PAVN rocket platoon was simultaneously firing their own cluster of rockets.

The white smoke and dust from the closest launch site mushroomed upward and was immediately visible. Sergeant Castilla's gunner opened fire on the position about 500 yards away as the rest of the platoon quickly spread out and began to move cautiously toward the enemy, approaching at various angles. There was no return fire, but it still took several minutes to cover the distance over the rough terrain. When they finally reached the site, all that remained were some bamboo rocket brackets and charred soil. The enemy, as so often the case in Vietnam, had mysteriously vanished into the hostile countryside.

There was no siren, no alert, no warning—just a bright flash followed instantaneously by a deafening explosion that transformed Ward 4 from an operating hospital into a pile of rubble. The lights went off momentarily throughout the compound until the emergency generators started up. The reduced power produced an eerie glow of light. The surrealistic sounds of the belated sirens blended with the haunting wails of the injured, mostly in monosyllabic Vietnamese.

Cannon Sample, a hospital corpsman, was watching a spectacular sunrise when he was blown out the door. After recovering from the initial shock of the blast, he found his path blocked by rubble and debris. He was forced to run around the building to another entrance while hospital personnel from other wards had already begun to work their way toward the injured.

JACK MEDLIN

Army personnel supervise the damage done by a 122-mm rocket after it hit Ward 4 during the early morning hours of June 8, 1969. A piece of shrapnel struck Sharon in the throat, killing her.

The ward's beds, once neatly lined up next to the walls, were mangled and shredded. An ocean of blood on the floor hampered the medical personnel as they threw aside the wreckage frantically looking for survivors. A 12-year-old Vietnamese child was found dead; 24 of the other patients had sustained additional injuries. In the corner, Lieutenant Sharon Lane lay motionless on the floor, her fatigues stained and soaked in blood and the pupils of her eyes dilated. There was a small shrapnel wound to her neck, but by the hospital's standards, it did not outwardly appear to be mortal. Dr. Brice Lippman, a doctor at the hospital was quoted in *The Army Reporter*, "I was walking to get some early coffee when I heard the explosion. I couldn't tell where the rocket had landed until I saw a number of Vietnamese running around crying. Then Lieutenant [Patricia] Carr took my arm, and we went into the shattered ward. Nurse Lane died within seconds of being hit by a piece of shrapnel which entered the throat."

In the emergency room, Lieutenant Sylvia Lutz had been taking advantage of the night's quietness by taking inventory when the first rocket hit the compound. In the ensuing commotion, several corpsmen burst into the emergency room carrying a stretcher containing Sharon's pale and limp body. The on-duty doctor immediately began to try to resuscitate her, but there were no vital signs, no blood pressure, no pulse. Lutz tried to start an intravenous drip but her efforts proved futile and an attempt at heart massage also failed. For the next several minutes, the concentrated efforts of the entire R&E centered around Sharon. It was obvious, however, despite all of the hospital's medical technology, there was nothing that could be done to revive her. A small piece of shrapnel had lacerated her carotid artery and she had died almost instantly.

By now, more casualties were pouring into the R&E. Another nurse had received a slight fragmentation wound as did a corpsman and a military policeman. The Vietnamese patients were more seriously hurt. To compound the chaos, several helicopters chose this inopportune time to arrive with more casualties evacuated from the field. One helicopter loaded with Viet Cong prisoners, though, was refused permission to land because of the circumstances and was directed to another hospital.

Lieutenant Lutz moved Sharon's body to the back of the emergency room and discreetly packed her neck wound. A privacy screen was strategically positioned immediately in front of the stretcher. Throughout the morning whenever time allowed, the doctors and nurses paid their respects to Sharon, standing before the screen, heads bowed in silent prayer. The 312th Evacuation Hospital had lost one of their own and, even in time of war, nurses were not supposed to die.

In Canton, Ohio, June 8 promised to be a beautiful, sunny spring day with the flowers in full bloom and temperatures predicted in the mid-70s. John Lane planned to use his day off working in the garage while his wife, Kay, was looking forward to watching the classic, *Pride of the Yankees*, on WKYC television at 3 P.M.

It was also the one-year anniversary of Robert F. Kennedy's burial at Arlington National Cemetery. In his honor, D.C. Stadium was going to be renamed R.F.K. Stadium during pregame ceremonies before the baseball game between the Washington Senators and Minnesota Twins. Most of the Kennedy clan was scheduled to be in attendance including the Kennedy's widow, Ethel, their children, and his sister-in-law, Jacqueline Kennedy Onassis. Also that morning the Canton *Repository* reported that the nation's banks had raised their prime interest rates to a record high of 8.5 percent and that college graduation exercises throughout the country were being disrupted by vocal antiwar demonstrations. Peace symbols, tie-dyed shirts, and sandals, were as prevalent as academic gowns and mortarboards. At Yale University, one student commencement speaker took advantage of the festivities to denounce the war in Southeast Asia.

Presidents Nixon and Thieu were concluding their meeting on Midway Island that same day. It was publicly announced that the United States would withdraw its first 25,000 troops within a matter of weeks, the first significant downsizing of American forces in years. At the same time, there were reports of a major increase in enemy activity throughout Vietnam. Just the previous day, there were 20 separate mortar and rocket attacks launched against American bases, including 7 attacks specifically targeting U.S. installations in the coastal areas located ominously near the hospital where the Lane's daughter, Sharon, was stationed. The U.S. Army meanwhile reported that 1,300 Communist troops were killed during the previous two days of fighting with American losses estimated at 100 killed and an additional 300 wounded. General Craighton Abrams maintained that the enemy activity was merely an aggravation and of little strategic value. He was quoted in the *Repository* as saying, "[The NVA are] just trying to harass and inflict casualties. I think the real purpose is psychological in terms of the people of the United States."

At 5:30 P.M., John and Kay Lane sat down in the family's living room to watch the evening news, the "McGee Report." The dominant story remained the Midway Island conference and the optimistic news of the impending first American troop withdrawals and its potential for breaking the deadlock in the Paris peace talks. Frank McGee also reported on the fighting in Vietnam, briefly noting that there had been an overnight enemy attack launched against the American base at Chu Lai. The casualties included some dead but no further details were available. Likewise, the 2nd Surgical Hospital at Lai Khi had been attacked by 122-mm rockets and the 247th Medical Detachment had come under 87-mm mortar fire during the night. Thirty-nine Americans died this day in Vietnam.

Mr. Lane, who had been resting on the sofa, sat upright immediately but said nothing. Chu Lai, after all, was a massive military complex. The chance of anything happening to Sharon was remote. Besides, she was safely stationed at a well-marked hospital of no military significance, and it was protected by every rule of engagement.

After the news was over, Mr. Lane went downstairs to the basement bathroom to take a shower so that he and his wife could go out for Sunday dinner. Just a few minutes later, an Army sedan drove up to the Lane's residence and a somber military officer got out and walked up to the front door. Mrs. Lane frantically called down to her husband, fearing that something dreadful had happened to Sharon. When she opened the door, all she could ask was, "Is she dead?" The officer replied simply, "Yes." With Mr. Lane now at her side, the officer awkwardly offered a few words of condolences but could provide no details or specifics about the circumstances of Sharon's death. When he finally left, the Lanes were alone with their grief—there was neither honor nor glory for being the parents of the only nurse to have been killed by hostile fire. All they felt was the overwhelming sense of loss and despair.

When the rocket attack began, most everyone at the 312th Evacuation Hospital was sleeping. Amy Lazar instinctively rolled under her bed at the BOQ for protection, bruising and cutting her eyebrow in the process. Lieutenant Leta Menton managed to seek safety in a bunker and sat out the attack in relative safety while Dr. Michael Carey pressed close to the concrete wall in the vacant operating room. After the all-clear sounded, word quickly spread of the hit on Ward 4 and of Sharon's death. For the first time, everyone stationed in Chu Lai felt vulnerable and afraid.

The ward had, in fact, sustained a direct hit by a Soviet-built 122-mm rocket. The immediate impact area was located in the shower and toilet facilities that linked the A and B wings together. The massive explosion destroyed 75 percent of the surrounding structures and seriously damaged much of its electrical wiring. A gaping hole had been opened in the ceiling, and dozens of pieces of shrapnel were embedded in the walls.

Navy Seabees arrived promptly on the scene at 0700 hours, just 65 minutes after the initial attack. They immediately roped off the entire area and carefully placed a tarp over the ward to deter gawkers and curiosity-seekers. Repairs began immediately. Amy Lazar recorded in her logbook, "The Seabees were here right away to start reconstruction. A miracle was involved as there were a number of 'hot' wires and the water pipe was broken. Had the two met, the resulting tragedy could have been horrible and a number of people electrocuted. Clean up went smoothly . . . although a gloom has set in."

Many people on the compound were in tears, while others walked aimlessly around in shock. Some at the hospital speculated openly that the black door to Sharon's quarters must have had some cosmic meaning, that perhaps she had some premonition of her death. In fact, the color choice had been predicated merely upon the minimal availability of paint at the supply depot. Other similar rumors began to circulate but few had any factual basis.

Later that day, Lieutenant Mary Metzinger and her boyfriend, Specialist Bill Smith, arrived back at Chu Lai after spending two weeks in Japan on R&R. Sharon had asked Mary to buy her a watch to replace the one she had lost earlier. When the couple arrived back at the hospital compound, they received confirmation of the attack and also learned the startling news of Sharon's death for the first time. Metzinger was stunned and could say little. She gave the money Sharon had entrusted to her to one of the nurses since she had been unable to buy the watch while on leave.

It would take several days before transportation could be arranged to return Sharon's body to the United States. In the meantime, the U.S. Army began to send a series of routine cables back to the Lanes concerning the disposition of her remains. The first arrived on Monday, June 9. It read:

> The Secretary of the Army has asked me to express his deep regret that your daughter, First Lieutenant Sharon A. Lane was killed in action in Vietnam on 8 June 1969, while on duty at the 312th Evacuation Hospital when the hospital came under rocket attack by a hostile force. Please accept my deepest sympathy. This confirms personal notification made by a representative of the Secretary of the Army.
>
> Kenneth G. Wickam, Major General

It was followed shortly by another telegram:

This concerns your daughter, 1Lt. Sharon A Lane. The Army will return your loved one to a port in the United States by first available military airlift. At the port remains will be placed in a metal casket and delivered (accompanied by a military escort) by most expeditious means to any funeral director designated by the next of kin or to any national cemetery in which there is available grave space. You will be advised by the United States port concerning the movement and arrival time at destination. Forms on which to claim authorized interment allowance will accompany the remains. This allowance may not exceed $75 if consignment is made directly to the superintendent of a national cemetery. When consignment is made to a funeral director prior to interment in a national cemetery. The maximum allowance is $250 if burial takes place in a civilian cemetery, the maximum allowance is $500 . . . Do not set date of funeral until port authorities notified you date and scheduled time of arrival.

On Tuesday, June 10, at 1100 hours, a memorial service was held in Sharon's memory at the 312th Evacuation Hospital's chapel. The doctors, in deference to Sharon's sacrifice, saw to it that all the nurses had seats of honor in the front of the chapel. The rest of the mourners crowded into the small structure to pay their respects. Chaplain Robert H. Love presided over the services with readings from the gospel of John. The congregation sang together the appropriate and soothing hymn, "Be Not Afraid." The hospital commander, Lieutenant Colonel Eston Caldwell, gave an appropriate memorial address.

Later that day, the Chu Lai Defense Command (CLDC) held a briefing for the entire hospital concerning the capabilities of the enemy. Both of the NVA rocket launch sites had been successfully located and destroyed by American forces. The meeting was designed primarily to reassure the staff and allay their fears. Amy Lazar, who attended the meeting wrote, "CLDC came to give us a talk on the defense of the Chu Lai compound from ground and

SYLVIA HOLLAND

The 312th Evacuation Hospital's chapel. Shortly after Sharon's death, a memorial service was held in her honor. The church was crowded with mourners with the nurses allowed to take seats in the front of the chapel.

rocket attack. They described the accuracy and nature of the 122-mm rocket. The number hitting the entire compound since February 7, 1969 was 127 . . . it was very informative and shows that ignorance breeds fear. We now know [that the rockets] have little accuracy with crude ways of launching the weapon."

The Surgeon General of the Army, Lieutenant General Leonard Heaton, wrote a letter of condolence to the Lanes in which he praised Sharon's performance while stationed at Chu Lai. He wrote, "Lt. Lane magnificently contributed in the care of our American soldiers as a distinguished member of the Army Medical Department team. Throughout the year she served her country, her record reflected exceptional capability in both clinical and administrative areas. Her personal characteristics and performance were described as . . . resourceful, flexibly, perceptive, very dependable, calm in emergency situations, and well organized in her work.' Her performance and devotion to duty not only brought credit to her but also to the Army Nurse Corps, the Army Medical Department, and the United States Army." Captain Lorraine Muntz noted in *The Army Reporter* that Sharon ". . . was an excellent nurse. She was always so kind to people and listened to them with compassion. She liked the Vietnamese, and they appreciated her tenderness and concern for them. After she had worked in the Vietnamese ward for about six weeks, I asked Missy Lane' (that was her nickname) if she would like a transfer . . . She replied that she liked it here and wanted to stay."

Almost immediately after the U.S. Army publicly released the news of Sharon's death, the press began to call the Lane's home incessantly, callously intruding on their private grief and agony. The death of the first American nurse to be killed as a direct result of enemy action was big news; virtually every major newspaper in the nation carried the story. A photograph of Sharon appeared in *Newsweek* magazine while one of the local papers, the *Alliance*, led its coverage with the banner headline, "Canton Army Nurse Killed in

Viet War." Mr. Lane finally issued a statement to the press in which he explained why his daughter had joined the Army and her motivation for going to Vietnam. The *Washington Star* quoted him as saying, "In her letters, [Sharon] said she wanted to help in Vietnam. It was a decision she made by herself and one that I did not question. She volunteered to serve in either South Vietnam or Korea."

Despite all the publicity, the exact circumstances surrounding Sharon's death were elusive. The Lanes were frustrated by the lack of specifics available through traditional U.S. Army sources. Some 48 hours after the attack, David Nelson, a male nurse who was stationed at Chu Lai, was finally able to get a phone call through to his father in Ohio and told him the complete story. Mr. Nelson immediately telephoned the Lane's and conveyed the precise details of their daughter's death. There was little to do now except make the final preparations for the funeral.

On June 12, the Lanes received yet another telegram, this time from the Commander of the Military Traffic Management and Terminal Service in California. The cable contained the specific flight schedules for the planes that would finally transport Sharon's body back to Ohio. First Lieutenant Rosemary Loria, a native of Cleveland who was an Army nurse stationed at Letterman Hospital, was detailed to serve as the official escort officer. Once informed of the final arrangements, Kay Lane's brother, who was residing in California, quickly made reservations to fly home on the same plane that would carry Sharon's coffin back to Canton.

United Flight 264 arrived at Canton-Dayton Airport as scheduled at 6:08 P.M., Friday, June 13th. A black hearse from the Kreighbaum Funeral Home was waiting. It had been just 51 days since Sharon had left from this same airport to go to Vietnam. At that time, no one expected that her homecoming would be marred by such anguish and grief. Neither did they imagine that she would return home as a grim statistic—the 78th person from Stark County, the 2,547th Ohioan, and the seventh American nurse to have died in the war.

The following day, at 10:00 A.M. visitation was scheduled for family and friends at Kreighbaum's. The U.S. Army Nurse Corps sent a high-level contingent from Washington, D.C led by Colonel Maude Smith. Doris Plastow and many of Sharon's other high school friends also crowded into the funeral home located immediately across the street from their beloved South Canton High School to pay their respects. At 1:00 P.M., the Pastor of the North Industry Methodist Church, Reverend John Jones, led the gathered mourners in a prayer service, reading from Isiah 53, "But He was wounded for our transgressions. He was bruised for our inequities, upon Him the chastisement that made us whole, and with His stripes we are healed."

After the brief services concluded, the mourners formed a motorcade outside the funeral home. Led by the hearse containing Sharon's body, a long line of cars followed closely with headlights on, up Interstate 77 through the city and past the Pro Football Hall of Fame into North Canton. Finally, the solemn procession turned onto Everhard Road and into the quiet, quiescent Sunset Hills Cemetery. On a hillside just inside the entrance, a tented gravesite had been neatly set up in Section 18. An Army casket team stood at attention while awaiting their arrival.

Sharon's family and friends got out of their vehicles and gathered together near the hearse. The six Army soldiers slowly removed Sharon's flag-draped coffin and carried it a short distance to the gravesite. After the committal prayers were offered, a military honor guard rendered a 21-gun salute and an Army bugler played "Taps." The casket team quickly and expertly folded the interment flag into a neat triangle and Lieutenant Loria presented the flag to Sharon's father, thanking him on behalf of President Nixon and the American people for his daughter's service to the United States. With that, the services were concluded and the mourners left the cemetery and Sharon's lonely, flower-strewn grave.

9

Aftermath

"[Sharon's] deep compassion and tenderness towards her Vietnamese patients were as important a contribution to peace as is the valor of our fighting men."

—President Richard M. Nixon, personal letter
(June 19, 1969)

On June 27, 1969, shortly after Sharon's burial in her hometown of Canton, *Life* magazine ran a photo essay entitled, "The Faces of the American Dead in Vietnam—One Week's Toll." The article featured the ghostly faces of the 242 Americans killed during the week of May 28, a veritable 12-page yearbook. For the first time, the magazine had successfully personalized the body count, a figure which was dutifully reported by all the nation's news media to measure the progress in the war. The accompanying story read in part, ". . . when the nation continues week after week to be numbered by a three-digit statistic which is translated to direct anguish in hundreds of homes all over the country, we must pause to look in to the faces. More than we must know *how many*, we must know *who*."

The war was continuing unabated in Vietnam, but President Nixon's orders to withdraw the first 25,000 American troops had an immediate and profound impact on the 312th Evacuation Hospital.

Since the reservists had already been slated for departure in mid-September, their date of departure was easily moved up two months to help accommodate Nixon's pledge without altering the strategic balance in the war or reducing American military capabilities.

By mid-July, the 91st Evacuation Hospital had assumed the operational responsibility for the Chu Lai hospital, while the North Carolinian reservists were freed from their medical duties to begin stowing away gear and preparing for their final departure from Vietnam. Two weeks later, on August 1, formal ceremonies were held for the unit on the tarmac of the adjacent U.S. Marine airbase while three military air-transports awaited nearby. Several speeches were given and medals awarded amid several banners bidding the reservists a fond *bon voyage* which were held aloft by attractive Vietnamese girls. Amy Lazar recounted in her logbook, "A very sad day as the 312th Evacuation Hospital departed for home after a rather nice ceremony at the airport. Several individuals were awarded the Vietnamese Cross of Gallantry . . . They left on three different C-141 planes at staggered times for security reasons . . . Many good friends [have] departed."

The unit safely reached the United States the following day after the marathon flight back to Fort Bragg, a full two months ahead of the original schedule. Within a short time, all the reservists had been mustered out of the U.S. Army and returned to civilian life. On August 6, the town of Winston-Salem held a welcoming home ceremony for them at the U.S. Army Reserve Center. Congressman Wilmer Mizell was in attendance as were several generals and the mayor of the city. The 312th's commander, Colonel Eston Caldwell praised his unit, claiming that they had been, ". . . the busiest medical evacuation hospital in Vietnam." He also said that the hospital had performed more surgical operations than any comparable unit in-country. A formal letter of commendation from Lieutenant General Frank T. Mildren followed. It read, "Throughout your service in Vietnam, the 312th provided life-giving professional medical services to the soldiers of the Americal Division. Your medical facility treated more than 9,800 patients and saw nearly 15,000 outpatients in a period of ten months—an outstanding record. Your ability to function as a smoothly working professional team greatly enhanced the vital medical support provided . . . and reflected favorably on the ability of reserve units to meet effectively the exacting challenges of a combat zone . . . I thank you for your efforts, sacrifices, and accomplishments in answering the call to active duty." Indeed, the 312th had proudly lived up to its division's motto, "Reserved for the Finest."

The nation had changed greatly during their one-year absence. Public support for the war evaporated after the 1968 Tet Offensive and even the so-called "silent majority" of middle-class Americans were growing increasingly weary of the fighting. Antiwar demonstrators conducted a daily vigil outside the gates of major military bases, chanting protest slogans and waving banners, while the returning soldiers were cautioned against wearing their fatigues into town least they provoke an unwanted confrontation.

The 312th Evacuation Hospital returned to its reserve status immediately after its return from Vietnam. The unit later moved its headquarters from Winston-Salem to new training facilities in Greensboro, North Carolina, on January 16th, 1980. Throughout this period, they continued to conduct regular, routine weekend training exercises.

In November 1990, three months after Iraq invaded Kuwait, President George Bush ordered the activation of the reserves and once again, the 312th was ready to answer the nation's call. A new generation of doctors, nurses, and corpsmen departed from Fort Bragg for the Middle East on January 20th, 1991, and served there for the next several months, caring primarily for Iraqi prisoners of war.

For the thousands of nurses who had freely volunteered to serve in Vietnam, their return to the United States proved to be a difficult transition for many. Their mission had been solely humanitarian, to help injured and wounded American GIs, and they had proudly served. Each had confronted death and catastrophic injury on a routine basis and had seen more human suffering than even the most battle-hardened veteran. Few civilians, however, seemed to understand these facts. The service and contributions of the U.S. Army Nurse Corps to the nation went largely unrecognized and unappreciated.

The Lanes continued to live quietly in South Canton. Both the United States and Vietnamese governments awarded Sharon several medals posthumously, including the Purple Heart, Bronze Star, Vietnam Service Medal, and Vietnamese Gallantry Cross. As the only nurse killed as a result of enemy action, Fitzsimons Army Hospital, where Sharon had been stationed initially before shipping overseas, recognized her sacrifice by dedicating the hospital's recovery room in her honor during Veteran's Day ceremonies held in November 1969. Major General James A. Wier unveiled a bronze plaque, which was placed outside the entrance to the intensive care unit. It read in part, "1st Lt. Sharon A. Lane, First Nurse Lost in Action, Republic of Vietnam—'Born to Honor—Ever at Peace'."

Shortly thereafter, plans were launched to commission a statue of Sharon in Canton to pay tribute to her and all of the 127 Stark County citizens killed during the war. The planned memorial was expected to cost $15,000, a substantial sum in the early 1970s. Collection cans were placed in businesses and shops throughout the city, while a grass-roots, door-to-door soliciting campaign simultaneously collected hundreds of dollars in small, private donations. A benefit country music concert and many fraternal and community organizations contributed to the successful fund-raising effort.

The seven-foot, bronze statue was sculpted by John M. Worthing, a local artist who had gained renown for casting busts of the athletes in the Pro Football Hall of Fame. The statue depicted Sharon in her military fatigues; it was one of the first Vietnam-era memorials in the United States. The dedication ceremonies were held on Memorial Day, May 28, 1973, and the monument was placed just outside the Aultman School of Nursing.

There would be many more ceremonies in Sharon's honor over the next several years; her parents dutifully attended most of them. For John Lane, though, the constant public recognition, even though well-meaning, only served to reinforce his personal, private

KAY LANE

The statue of Sharon Lane on the grounds of Aultman Hospital in Canton, Ohio. The monument was dedicated on Memorial Day, 1973 and was one of the nation's first Vietnam-era memorials.

anguish. Sharon, in death, had unintentionally become a symbol to many, but to her father, she was still his little girl and was now gone forever. He died in 1979, a decade after Sharon, having never fully accepted his loss. He was appropriately buried in a grave adjacent to Sharon's at the Sunset Hills Memorial Park cemetery in North Canton.

By January, 1973, a fragile peace agreement had been negotiated by the United States which required the removal of all American combat forces in return for the return of all American prisoners of war and a cease fire in Vietnam. Still, the North was allowed to maintain a massive military presence below the 17th parallel which included an estimated 120,000 combat troops in the I-Corps sector alone.

In the spring 1975, the North Vietnamese launched a massive military offensive with the goal of capturing Saigon by May 1st. Without American air-support, ARVN forces were quickly routed throughout South Vietnam by the onslaught of superior enemy forces. President Nguyen Van Thieu ordered the abandoning of the provinces of Quang Tri, Tua Thien, Quang Nam, Quang Tin, and Quang Ngai to redeploy his dwindling forces further to the south. Chu Lai was abandoned on March 26th and just a few days later, Da Nang fell to the North Vietnamese.

Faced with the imminent collapse of the South, President Gerald R. Ford ordered the American military to assist with the evacuation of the U.S. embassy and to begin the humanitarian airlift of loyal South Vietnamese civilians to safety. He also initiated, *Operation Babylift* which was designed to repatriate hundreds of Vietnamese orphans to foster homes within the United States.

The first C-5A Galaxy flew into Saigon from Clark Air Force Base on April 4th, 1975 amid the chaos and panic surrounding the raging North Vietnamese offensive. The C-5 was a relatively new addition to the U.S. Air Force's arsenal and was a massive transport with enormous airlift capabilities. It had been plagued, though, with serious problems during its recent development and had yet to be tested in a combat situation. A medical flight crew consisting of three aeromedical evacuation technicians and two flight nurses, Lieutenant Harriet Goffinett and Captain Mary Klinker, were already on the scene at Tan Son Nhut airport. The group was not detailed initially to help with the emergency evacuation of hundreds of waiting Vietnamese children. Captain Klinker requested and received permission to assist with the airlift of the orphans and to assist them in reaching safety in the Philippines.

Most of the children were mere infants who were quickly loaded into the cargo bay and troop compartment of the C-5 aircraft. Since there were few seats on-board, the youngest children were placed in small boxes that were carefully positioned in rows of ten, and then strapped down to the deck of the plane. Captain Klinker was assigned to the cargo bay area to assist with the care of the children while in-flight.

The plane's takeoff from Saigon was uneventful, but suddenly at 23,000 feet, its cargo door blew off causing a rapid decompression of the aircraft. The pilot skillfully turned the plane around in an attempt to return to Tan Son Nhut. The cargo bay portion of the plane, however, had sustained serious damage and several people were gravely injured in the accident. Captain Klinker, disregarding her own safety, heroically administered oxygen and cared for an unconscious sergeant while the other crew members quickly and calmly prepared for a crash landing.

The plane impacted in a rice paddy just two miles short of the runway and broke into several pieces after the crash. The cargo area was virtually destroyed and had the highest casualties; 96 of the 102 children died upon impact. Mary Klinker and 10 other crew members were also killed. Thus, she became the eighth and final American nurse to die in Vietnam.

Typhoon Hester crashed into the central Vietnamese coast in October 1971, its powerful winds and drenching rains causing massive

destruction throughout the entire I-Corps region. The 91st Evacuation Hospital, with its exposed location sustained major damage as
did the buildings of the adjacent Americal Division. Rather than
rebuilding the bases during a period of major American troop withdrawals, the facilities were instead turned over to the Army of the
Republic of Vietnam. The Americal Division held stand-down ceremonies later that month, finally furling their flags and division
banners for the last time, while the 91st Evacuation Hospital con-
currently ceased hospital operations. They departed Vietnam on
November 29th and, for the first time since 1967, there was no
significant U.S. Army base at Chu Lai.

After the war, Chu Lai once again became a small, inconsequen-
tial hamlet. The North Vietnamese had seized all the military equipment left behind during the hasty retreat from the compound in
March 1975, while local residents plundered the empty base for the
remaining scrap iron and supplies. Le Ly Hayslip, the author of
Heaven and Earth, wrote, "I have driven by Chu Lai, and I was
surprised to find that nothing is there. If the local people hadn't
told me that site was the [base], I would never have known there
was one . . . Chu Lai was on the sandy beaches of the China Sea,
where it was always windy. After the North Vietnamese came, the
villagers took everything that was left by the U.S. army for their
personal use. Then when everything was gone, the waves pulled
everything into the sea, and now there is nothing left." The once
mighty American presence in the region has all but disappeared,
having been reclaimed slowly by wind, sea, and scavenger.

For years after the collapse of South Vietnam, the American public
seemed intent on forgetting all about the war in a type of collective,
historical amnesia. It was not until 1982, fully nine years after the
last American combat troops had been withdrawn from Vietnam,
that a memorial was dedicated in Washington, D.C., to all those
who had served during the nation's longest war. It was designed by
Maya Lin, a 20-year old architect student at Yale University who

successfully captured the agony of the war. The memorial consists of a series of stark black panels in the shape of a *V*. The memorial lists the names of all 58,191 Americans who died in Southeast. Sharon's name is listed on Panel 23W of the wall.

Two years later, a bronze monument depicting three combat soldiers was added to the memorial site. Diane Carlson Evans, a U.S. Army nurse who served in Vietnam from 1968 through 1969, believed that a similar statue should be erected nearby to pay similar tribute to nurses and all women who served during the Vietnam era. In an article for *Vietnam* magazine, author Sally Eauclaire explained, ". . . many journalists and government officials mistakenly thought that there were very few women in Vietnam—'only' eight had died, after all—that they worked in 'safe' areas and overall contributed very little. 'Sometimes I could not believe the stupid questions,' Evans remembers, I had to learn to keep my dignity and educate them. The fact is there were no safe areas in Vietnam. Women were shot at. There were no such things as frontline and rear areas.' In constant danger, and working for days with minimal sleep, the nurses confronted such hideous wounds that they often questioned the value of their work."

Evans began an intensive personal lobbying campaign to obtain Congressional approval for the addition. With the support of virtually all major veterans' organizations, her grass-roots effort finally succeeded. Ground-breaking ceremonies for the monument were held in July 1993.

Glenna Goodacre was commissioned to sculpt the monument. She explained her concept in the dedication program, "My first concern in designing this sculpture was to arrange the four figures in a composition that is interesting from all angles . . . it seemed natural for a nurse—in a moment of crisis—to be supported by sandbags as she serves as the life-support for a wounded soldier lying across her lap. The standing woman looks up, in search of a [medevac] helicopter or, perhaps, in search of help from God. The kneeling figure has been called the heart and soul' of the piece because so many vets see themselves in her. She stares at an empty helmet, her posture reflecting her despair, frustrations, and all of

The grave of Lieutenant Sharon A. Lane at the Sunset Hills Memorial Cemetery, Canton, Ohio.

the horrors of war . . . I can only hope that future generations who view the sculpture will stand in tribute to these women who served during the Vietnam era."

The Vietnam Women's Memorial was dedicated during Veteran's Day ceremonies in 1993. Thousands of nurses, Red Cross workers, civilians, and GIs from all over the country attended the special services. The American people, likewise, were finally beginning to appreciate the many contributions of women to the war effort.

Thousands of tourists to Washington continue to visit the Vietnam Memorial each month. Most pause and reflect at the gleaming, black panels inscribed with the thousands of names of the American dead. It is a humbling and overwhelming experience since each inscription represents a life cut short by the war. As the tourists and pilgrims exit to the east, they are confronted by Goodacre's magnificent bronze statue and, for many, it is their first realization that thousands of women also served in Vietnam and that some died there as well.

Some 700 miles to the northwest, there is yet another Vietnam memorial, although it is not listed in any tourist manual or guidebook. Over the last 25 years, Canton's urban sprawl has transformed the once-quiet Erlich Road into a major highway that carries thousands of commuters daily to work. At its intersection with Interstate 77, there is a large shopping complex and dozens of hotels. Across the street from the Arby's fast-food restaurant is a modest, iron gate at the entrance onto the grounds of the Sunset Hills Memorial Cemetery. Once inside, the hectic pace of modern life is immediately replaced by a sense of peace, serenity, and eternity. Midway up the first sloping hill in the section, known as the "Garden of the Christus," there is a flat, bronze memorial marker. It is tarnished and dull with age but nevertheless remains a poignant reminder of the human toll of the Vietnam War. It reads simply:

Lt. Sharon A. Lane
July 7, 1943
June 8, 1969
Killed on Duty in Vietnam

APPENDIX A

American Hospitals in Vietnam

DECEMBER 1968

Surgical Hospitals
2nd Surgical (Lai Khe)
3rd Surgical (Dong Tam)
7th Surgical (Xuan Loc)
18th Surgical (Camp Evans)
22nd Surgical (Phu Bai)
27th Surgical (Chu Lai)
45th Surgical (Tay Ninh)

Evacuation Hospitals
12th Evac (Cu Chi)
24th Evac (Long Binh)
29th Evac (Can Tho)
36th Evac (Vung Tau)
67th Evac (Qui Nhon)
71st Evac (Pleiku)
85th Evac (Phu Bai)

91st Evac (Tuy Hoa)
93rd Evac (Long Binh)
95th Evac (Da Nang)
312th Evac (Chu Lai)

Field Hospitals
3d Field Hospital (Saigon)
8th Field Hospital (Nha Trang)
17th Field Hospital (An Khe)
74th Field Hospital (Long Binh)
311th Field Hospital (Qui Nhon)

Convalescent Center
6th Convalescent Center (Cam
Ranh Bay)[1]

---

[1]The Convalescent Center at Cam Ranh Bay was the largest American medical facility in Vietnam with a capacity of over 1,300 patients. By December, 1968, there was a total of 5,283 hospital beds available. See Lt. General Carroll H. Dunn, *Vietnam Studies: Base Development in South Vietnam—1965-1970*. (Washington, DC: Department of the Army, 1972), pp. 76–78.

APPENDIX B

Lt. Sharon A. Lane's Last Letter from Vietnam

JUNE 4, 1969

Dear Mom and Dad,

Got your letter of the 28th, Mom, yesterday, 3 June. Today I got Dad's of 26th April. You never know what is going on with the mail. Haven't gotten the packages yet. Heaven only knows when they will arrive and in what condition. You should see some.

Wrote Gladys and Grandma a note on May 31st, so they should be getting it soon.

[I] worked in ICU again today. [I] was lucky [since] it got to 102°, and ICU is air-conditioned. They have a lot of really sick patients. Had three die yesterday. They still have four on respirators. None too good, either.

One of the GIs who died yesterday was from Ward 8, medical. [He] had malaria. During the previous night, he had been nauseated and kept getting up to go to the latrine to vomit. He got up at 2 AM and was running to the latrine. [He] ran into a water cooler which threw him backwards [and] fell really hard and cracked his head on the cement floor. The nurse who was on duty said you could *hear* his skull fracture. He immediately started bleeding from the ears and nose and stopped breathing. Then had cardiac arrest. They got him going again and transferred him to ICU but he died anyway yesterday. [He] had severe brain damage. [The] other death was a GI with multiple fragment wounds from a mine explosion. He was there two weeks ago when I worked that other day in ICU. Also a Vietnamese died but I don't know what was wrong with him.

Census hit the 10,000 mark yesterday. This unit, the 312th, has treated 10,000 patients since they arrive last Sept. Unbelievable. Registrar office had a poll going as to what time and what state the 10,000th patient would be admitted. Was yesterday morning. Haven't heard who won the money yet.

They put plastic or rubber floor tile down in the mess hall the evening before last. Looked real nice until yesterday noon when it got hot. The tar came up between the tile and it got tracked all over the place. Couldn't move your chair at all. It was stuck to the floor. Really got hot today, too. Hate to think of July and August.

How did the home-made ice cream turn out?

Start "nights" tomorrow so don't have to get up early tomorrow. Nice thought.

Still very quiet around here. Haven't gotten mortared for [a] couple of weeks now. We are getting some new nurses this week. They are from the unit who will take over when the 312th goes home in Sept. Their hospital is farther south somewhere. They are handling 80% Vietnamese casualties now so are turning their hosp[ital] over to the Viets and coming here to take over. Suppose to get the new chief nurse tomorrow. So the unit will change names in Sept. Forget what unit they are. However, they are suppose to be an RA (regular army) group. Not a reserve unit like the 312th is. Things are suppose to get a lot more "strict army style." No one is looking forward to it.

Read a book last night and missed a good Lee Marvin movie at the mess hall.

Had a movie star visit here the 2nd or 3rd week I was here. Named Ricardo Montaban (sic)?? Ever hear of him? Forgot to mention it previously. Some of the older people here remembered him. Said he was in movies with Ester Williams.

Will stop for now. Getting sleepy.

See you sooner.

Shar

APPENDIX C

Damage Report of Rocket Attack on the 312th Evacuation Hospital

10 JUNE 1969

Subject: Damages Sustained During Rocket Attack

Commanding Officer
44th Medical Battalion
APO 96325

1. At approximated 0550 hours on 8 June 1969 one 122 mm rocket impacted directly on Ward 4A and 4B. The following damages and personnel injuries resulted:

   a. Total of 2 people killed.

      (1) 1LT Sharon Lane ANC—open fragment wound of neck.

      (2) 12 year old Vietnamese girl—fragment wound of neck.

   b. Total of 27 people injured.

      (1) 1 Nurse, ANC—minor fragment wounds.

      (2) 1 Corpsman 91B20—fragment wounds of leg and wrist.

      (3) 1 me MP Corps—fragment wounds of hip and thigh.

      (4) 24 Vietnamese patients on Ward received various fragment wounds.

      (5) Only 1 GI hospitalized as result of attack (Corpsman 91B20).

c. Wards 4A and 4B 75% destroyed.
   (1) Showers, toilet facilities completely destroyed.
   (2) Roofs of 4A and 4B 30% destroyed.
   (3) 2 ice boxes destroyed.
   (4) Electrical wiring and outlets 50% destroyed.
   (5) NSAD began repairs to Ward 4 at 0700 on 8 June 69—completion expected by 0700 11 June 1969.

d. Damages to Hospital and Detachment Headquarters.
   (1) Fragments thru walls and ceilings.
   (2) 3 file cabinets damaged by fragments.
   (3) 1 desk damaged by fragments.

e. Following reports were prepared.
   (1) USARV Forms 130-R for injured personnel were furnished your headquarters 8 June 1969.
   (2) DD Form 1076—Record of Personal Effects for 1LT Sharon Lane.
   (3) Letter of sympathy to 1LT Lane's family signed by LTC Caldwell.
   (4) Letter of condolence to 1LT Lane's family for signature of CO, 44th Med Bde.
   (5) 44th Med Bde form 109 (Posthumous Award Feeder Report) on 1LT Lane furnished your Headquarters 9 June 1969.
   (6) DD Form 200 (Report of Survey) on equipment loss furnished your headquarters 10 June 1969.
   (7) USARV Form 130-R (ETHER Report) on 1LT Lane.

f. Memorial services were held 1100 hours on 10 June 1969 in 312th Evac Hosp Chapel by Chaplain (CPT) Love for 1LT Lane.

g. Ward 4A and 4B is expected to be operational by 0700 11 June 69.

h. Attached is sketch of Ward 4A and 4B and rocket impact location as Inclosure 1.

FOR THE COMMANDER:

[Signed]
CLYDE E. WELCH
CPT, MSC
Adjutant

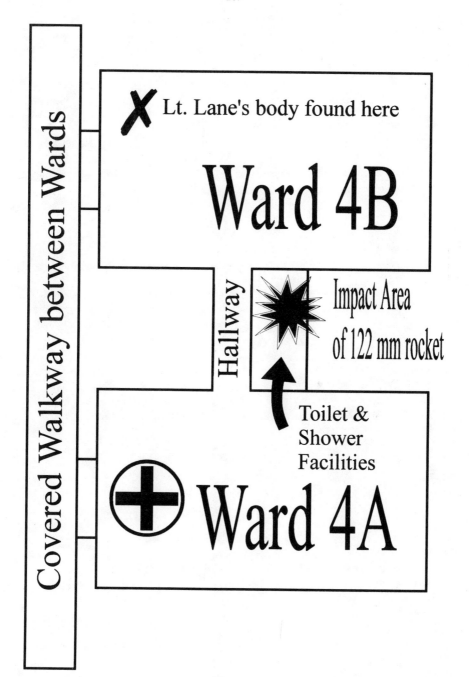

Covered Walkway between Wards

Lt. Lane's body found here

Ward 4B

Hallway

Impact Area
of 122 mm rocket

Toilet &
Shower
Facilities

Ward 4A

APPENDIX D

Listing of Americans Killed in Vietnam

JUNE 8, 1969[1]

CPL. James D. Adkins, age 21
PFC. Gale L. Barnes, age 20
LTC. Don L. Bartley, age 36
LCPL. David L. Bell, age 21
LCPL. Paul M. Bowlin, age 21
SGT. David Brown, age 20
SSGT. Kenneth E. Enfinger, age 29
PFC. Jerry L. Ervin, age 21
SSGT. Glenn R. Fleitman, age 20
LCPL. William H. Green, age 20
PFC. Michael W. Hagie, age 19
PH2. Carl W. Hudgins, age 24
CWO. Dale L. Johnson, age 24
PFC. Jay A. Kaufman, age 26
2LT. Carl J. Keahey, age 24
LCPL. Keo J. Keshner, age 21
CPL. George F. Landi, age 20
1LT. Sharon A. Lane, age 25
PFC. Robert N. Latimer, age 25
PFC. Malcolm F. Leger, age 20

CPL. John E. Lorence, age 22
PFC. Melville A. Lurth, age 23
SP4. George F. Martinez, age 33
PFC. Herman R. Morris, age 18
PFC. David L. McKee, age 18
1LT. Ronald W. McLean, age 24
WO. Albert D. Owens, age 21
PFC. James A. Person, age 21
PFC. Johnny B. Robertson Jr., age 23
SGT. Robert R. Sheridan, age 25[2]
PFC. Deane F. Smith, Jr., age 20
CPL. Thomas W. Strathmann, age 22
PH1. Robert G. Stricklin, age 26
CPL. Terry E. Toole, age 22
SP5. Ignacio L. Villalobos, age 22
PFC. Roy L. Walker, age 21
JO1. William R. Wilson, age 27
CPL. Robert A. Wimer, age 19
LCPL. Rober L. Young, age 22

[1]39 Americans were killed in Vietnam on June 8, 1969. They came from 20 different states including three from Ohio.
[2]Sgt. Robert Sheridan from Central Islip, New York, was killed on his 25th birthday.

171

APPENDIX E

American (Female) Nurses Who Died in Vietnam

Capt. Eleanor Grace Alexander
Born: 18 September 1940
Commenced RVN Tour: 6 June 1967
Died: 30 November 1967

2nd Lt. Pamela Dorothy Donovan
Born: 25 March 1942
Commenced RVN Tour: 10 April 1968
Died: 8 July 1968

2nd Lt. Carol Ann Elizabeth Drazba
Born: 11 December 1943
Commenced RVN Tour: 13 October 1965
Died: 18 February 1966

Ltc. Annie Ruth Graham
Born: 7 November 1916
Commenced RVN Tour: 16 November 1967
Died: 14 August 1968

2nd Lt. Elizabeth Ann Jones
Born: 12 September 1943
Commenced RVN Tour: 13 October 1965
Died: 18 February 1966

Capt. Mary Therese Klinker
Born: 3 October 1947
Commenced RVN Tour: NA
Died: 4 April 1975

1st Lt. Sharon Ann Lane
Born: 7 July 1942
Commenced RVN Tour: 24 April 1969
Died: 8 June 1969

1st Lt. Diane Orlowski
Born: 13 April 1944
Commenced RVN Tour: 27 January 1967
Died: 30 November 1967

---

[1]Ltc. Graham suffered a subarachnoid hemorrhage while serving with the 91st Evacuation Hospital in Tuy Hoa. She was air-evaced to Japan and died there three days later.

SELECTED
CHRONOLOGY

1943

July 7   Sharon Lane is born in Ohio.

1960

Dec. 20   The National Liberation Front (Viet Cong) is officially or-
              ganized by the Hanoi government to wage guerrilla warfare
              in the South.

1961

May 31   Sharon Lane graduates from South Canton High School.

Fall   The Kennedy administration escalates American involve-
              ment in the war in Southeast Asia by sending hundreds of
              advisers to aid and help in the training of ARVN forces.

1962

March   The 8th Field Hospital commences operations in Nha Trang
              becoming the first American hospital in Vietnam.

1964

Aug. 4   American destroyers are allegedly attacked by North Vietnamese torpedo boats in the Gulf of Tonkin. The incident leads to Congress passing the Gulf of Tonkin Resolution which gives the President broad war-making powers in Southeast Asia.

Dec. 24   Four US Navy nurses are wounded in a terrorist attack launched by the Viet Cong against the Brink BOQ in Saigon. They are the first female casualties of the war and all receive the Purple Heart.

1965

March 2   Operation *Rolling Thunder* commences.

March 9   The first American combat troops land at DaNang.

April 7   Lyndon Johnson delivers a major foreign policy address on the war in Southeast Asia at Johns Hopkins University.

April 17   15,000 anti-war demonstrators protest the escalation of the war in Washington, D.C.

April 25   Sharon Lane graduates from the Aultman School of Nursing.

May 7   Navy Seabees stake out a runway at Chu Lai, South Vietnam.

June 1   The first air operations are launched from the new airfield at Chu Lai.

July 3   The 8,000 foot jet-capable runway at Chu Lai is completed and fully operational.

Dec. 31   United States troop strength in Vietnam soars to 385,300 troops; 6,644 Americans have been killed in the war.

1966

Feb. 18   2nd Lt. Carol Drazba and 2nd Lt. Elizabeth Ann Jones are killed in a helicopter accident near Saigon. They are the first two nurses killed in Vietnam.

1967

April 26   The US Marines turn over primary responsibility for the Chu Lai base to the Army. The Marines continue to operate the airfield.

May 8   The 2nd Surgical Hospital is transferred from An Khe to Chu Lai and establishes the first medical facility in the region.

Sept. 25   The 54th Medical Detachment begins helicopter dust-off operations from Chu Lai in support of the Americal Division.

Nov. 30   Capt. Eleanor Alexander and 1st Lt. Diane Orlowski are killed in the crash of a C-47 aircraft near Qui Nhon.

1968

Jan. 30   The Tet Offensive begins with an all out assault on American and South Vietnamese strongholds.

Feb. 17   The United States sustains its highest weekly casualties of the war with 543 Americans killed in action and 2,547 wounded.

March 27   The 27th Surgical Hospital arrives at Chu Lai.

March 31   President Lyndon Johnson announces to the nation that he will not seek re-election.

April 8   President Johnson orders the mobilization of some 20,000 reservists, the first such call-up since the Berlin crisis of 1961.

April 18   The 27th Surgical Hospital becomes fully operational.

May 2   Sharon Lane is commissioned as a 2nd Lieutenant.

May 13   The 312th Evacuation Hospital departs Winston-Salem, North Carolina for training at Fort Benning, Georgia.

June 14   1st Lt. Sharon Lane graduates from basic training at Fort Sam Houston, Texas.

June 16   Lt. Lane arrives at her first duty assignment, Fitzsimons Hospital in Denver, Colorado.

July 7   Sharon Lane quietly celebrates her 25th birthday while stationed at Fitzsimons Hospital.

July 8   A female nurse assigned to the 85th Field Evacuation Hospital in Qui Nhon dies from a self-inflicted overdose of barbiturates. Official records describe the cause of her death as "Self destruction while mentally unsound."

July 12-14   John and Kay Lane visit their daughter in Colorado.

Aug. 14   Lt. Col. Ruth Graham, a 52-year old veteran of World War II, dies of a stroke while working at the 91st Evacuation Hospital in Tuy Hoa.

Aug. 30   Sharon Lane is promoted to the rank of 1st Lieutenant.

Sept. 23   The 312th Evacuation Hospital arrives at Chu Lai to relieve the 2nd Surgical Hospital which was being redeployed to An Khe.

Sept. 28	The Commanding General of the 44th Medical Brigade visits the 312th Evacuation Hospital to welcome them in-country.
Sept. 30	U.S. troop strength in Vietnam reaches 537,800 soldiers.
Oct. 1	The 312th Evacuation Hospital commences operations in support of the Americal division.
Nov. 5	Richard M. Nixon is elected President of the United States on a pledge to honorably bring an end to the war in Vietnam.
Nov. 16	Colin Powell, an officer with the Americal Division, is treated at the 312th for injuries sustained in a helicopter crash.
Dec. 18-21	The base at Chu Lai is hit 14 times by enemy 140-mm rockets.
Dec. 24	Bob Hope performs at the Special Services Amphitheater at Chu Lai before thousands of appreciative troops.
Dec. 31	American troop strength reaches 536,100 soldiers; 30,610 Americans have died in Vietnam.

1969

Feb. 22	American troop strength in Vietnam peaks at 542,500.
Feb. 23	The 312th Evacuation Hospital HEADQUARTERS building is hit by enemy rocket fire as North Vietnamese troops launch a series of coordinated attacks throughout the South.
Feb. 26	The entire Chu Lai area is attacked by some 61 enemy rockets killing 11 and wounding 156.
March 5	Secretary of Defense Melvin Laird visits Saigon in an effort to reassess American military policy in Vietnam; he concludes that the United States must begin a phased withdrawal of forces and to "Vietnamize" the war.
April 6	Sharon Lane leaves Fitzsimons Hospital for two weeks leave before shipping out to Vietnam.
April 24	A TWA MAC-PAC flight leaves Travis Air Force Base at 2030 hours with 1st Lt. Lane.
April 26	Sharon Lane reports for duty at Long Binh, Republic of Vietnam.
April 29	Sharon Lane arrives at the 312th Evacuation Hospital in Chu Lai at 1700 hours.
May 4	Lt. Lane is assigned to the Vietnamese Ward at the hospital.
May 10	Chu Lai is attacked by enemy fire; Lt. Lane sleeps through the entire episode.

May 11-12	North Vietnamese troops launch 159 rockets against US military bases throughout South Vietnam.
May 12	A NVA 122 mm rocket strikes the 312th Evacuation Hospital blowing up a sailboat in an unusual mid-morning attack (1000 hours).
May 13	President Richard M. Nixon proposes legislation to revise the current selective service system in an effort to make it more equitable.
May 15	At the University of California, Berkeley, rioting erupts between students and the National Guard as California authorities attempt to close down the so-called "People's Park" on campus.
May 18	Chu Lai is attacked by enemy rockets and mortars; all shots fall harmlessly into the South China Sea.
May 19	Ho Chi Minh's 79th birthday.
May 20	Rockets are fired against the Chu Lai compound; most struck the beach to the south or fell harmlessly into the South China Sea.
May 22	Ricardo Montalban visits the 312th.
May 31	The Americal Division reports that for the month, 707 NVA troops were killed while American LZ's took 490 rounds of enemy mortar fire.
June 3	The 312th Evacuation Hospital treats its 10,000 patient in just 245 days since its arrival in Vietnam.
June 4	Sharon writes what is to be her last letter home.
June 8	A 122 mm rocket strikes the Vietnamese Ward at the 312th Evacuation Hospital killing 1st Lt. Sharon Lane. President Richard Nixon announces the first American troop withdrawals from Vietnam. Thirty-nine Americans are killed in Vietnam.
June 10	A memorial service is held for Lt. Lane at the 312th Evacuation Hospital chapel.
June 13	A casket containing Sharon Lane's remains arrives back home in Canton, Ohio.
July 8	The U.S. 9th Infantry Division becomes the first unit to leave Vietnam under President Nixon's plan for a phased withdrawal of American forces.
August 1	The 312th Evacuation Hospital leaves Vietnam after 312 days in-country.

August 2   Members of the 312th Evacuation Hospital arrive back in Winston-Salem, North Carolina.

August 7   The 312th is de-activated and the reservists are allowed to return to their civilian jobs and occupations.

Sept. 3   Ho Chi Minh dies.

Oct. 15   The Vietnam Moratorium is held in Washington, D.C.

Nov. 11   The ICU ward at Fitzsimons Hospital is renamed the Lane Recovery Suite in honor of Lt. Lane.

Dec. 31   The United States has lost 44,224 Americans killed in Vietnam.

1970

May 4   Four students are killed and nine wounded during anti-war protest at Kent State University in Ohio.

1971

Oct. 23-24 Typhoon Hester slams into the coast of South Vietnam killing 100 and heavily damaging the Americal Division Headquarters and the 91st Evacuation Hospital at Chu Lai.

Oct. 29   American troop strength in Vietnam drops to 196,000, the lowest total since January, 1968.

Nov. 12   President Richard M. Nixon announces the withdrawal of 45,000 American troops. Casualties have been reduced to fewer than 10 killed per week and U.S. troops are no longer engaged in offensive ground action.

Nov. 29   The 91st Evacuation Hospital leaves Chu Lai; the American base is turned over to the Army of the Republic of Vietnam.

1972

March 29   The last contingent of American nurses leave Vietnam; over 5,000 nurses served during the war. Their average age was 23.6 years old.

Aug. 11   The last American combat troops are withdrawn from Vietnam.

1973

Jan. 27   A cease fire agreement is reached in Paris between the United States and the North Vietnamese.

Feb. 14   The first American prisoners of war are released by Hanoi.

1975

March 14   President Thieu orders all ARVN forces to evacuate the Central Highlands and the Northern Provinces causing panic and chaos among troops and civilians.

March 29   DaNang falls to the Communist.

April 4   An Air Force C-5A crashes shortly after take-off during Operation *Babylift* killing over 300 infants and military personnel; Capt. Mary Klinker perishes, the last American nurse to die in Vietnam.

April 30   Saigon falls to the Communists.

1982

Nov. 11   The Vietnam Memorial is dedicated in Washington, D.C. It lists all of the names of the 58,182 American soldiers, servicemen, and nurses who died during the Vietnam War.

1984

May 25   The Vietnam Unknown Soldier is laid to rest at Arlington National Cemetery. President Ronald Reagan eulogized, "A grateful nation opens her heart today in gratitude for [the Vietnam veterans'] sacrifice, for their courage and their noble service."

1990

Nov. 20   President George Bush activates the 312th Evacuation Hospital for service in the Persian Gulf.

1991

Jan. 20   The 312th Evacuation Hospital arrives in Southwest Asia.

Feb. 14   The hospital begins medical operations in support of the ongoing land war.

May 29   The 312th Evacuation Hospital is deactivated after its service in the Persian Gulf War.

1993

Nov. 11   The Vietnam Women's Memorial is dedicated in Washington, D.C. to all those who served during the Vietnam conflict.

SELECTED
BIBLIOGRAPHY

The following libraries, archives, and repositories were visited during the research and prepartion for this book: the National Archives Cartographic and Still Pictures branches (College Park, Maryland); the United States Army Military Institute (Carlisle, Pennsylvania); the Center for Military History (Washington, D.C.); the National Archives Military Records Center (Suitland, Maryland); the Wake Forrest University Library (Winston-Salem, North Carolina); the Historian's Office at Travis Air Force Base (Fairfield, California); the Gerald R. Ford Library at the University of Michigan (Ann Arbor, Michigan); and the Canton Public Library (Canton, Ohio).

23rd Infantry (Americal) Division. Operational Reports/Lessons Learned: Army War College (Carlisle, Pa.).

44th Medical Brigade. Operational Reports/Lessons Learned: Army War College (Carlisle, Pa.).

44th Medical Brigade Daily Staff Journals. National Archives and Records Service (Suitland, Md.). RG-472 Box 6: Jan. 1969–Dec. 1969; RG-472 Box 1: May 1966-Dec. 1969.

"Army Nurse Killed by Enemy Rocket," *The Army Reporter*. June 23, 1969, p. 1.

"Army Nurse Killed in War," Washington *Star*, June 10, 1969, p. 1.

Becker, Marilyn. Telephone Interview. October 6, 1994.

Bellamy, Dwight. Telephone Interview. August 29, 1994.

Bergerud, Eric M. *Red Thunder, Tropic Lightning: The World of a Combat Division in Vietnam*. Boulder: Westview Press, 1993.

Bilton, Michael and Kevin Sim. *Four Hours in My Lai*. New York: Viking Press, 1992.

Booz, Elizabeth B. and Sarah Jessup, trans. *Vietnam: Land of the Ascending Dragon*. Lincolnwood, Il.: Passport Books, 1992.

Bowman, John ed. *The Vietnam War: An Almanac*. New York: Bison Books Corp., 1985.

Caldwell, LTC. Eston R. Narrative Description for Bronze Star for Lt. Sharon A. Lane.

"Canton Army Nurse Killed in Viet War," *Alliance*, June 10, 1969, p. 1.

Carey, Dr. Michael. Personal Interview (New Orleans, La.). Feb. 18, 1995.

Carey, Dr. Michael. Telephone Interview. January 19, 1995.

Castilla, Rick. Personal Letter to Kay Lane, May 18, 1993.

Castilla, Rick. Telephone Interview, Nov. 22, 1994.

Clarke, Jeffrey J. *Advice and Support: The Final Years—The US Army in Vietnam*. Washington, D.C.: Center for Military History, 1988.

Colomb, Erin. "The Nurses Saw More Gore . . .". *Vietnam* Magazine. February, 1995, pp. 16, 18-19.

Crossland, LTC Richard B. and Major James T. Currie. *Twice the Citizen: A History of the United States Army Reserve, 1908–1983*. Washington, D.C.: Office of the Chief, Army Reserve, 1984.

Divito, Penny (Lopez). Telephone Interview. January 6, 1994.

Dunn, Lt. Gen. Carroll H. *Vietnam Studies: Base Development in South Vietnam—1965–1970*. Washington, D.C.: Department of Army, 1972.

Ebert, James R. *A Life in a Year: The American Infantryman in Vietnam, 1965–1972*. Novato, CA.: Presidio Press, 1993.

Eauclaire, Sally. "Sculpting a Vision," *Vietnam* Magazine, Dec. 1993, pp. 22–28.

Faith, William Robert. *Bob Hope: A Life in Comedy*. New York: G.P Putnam's Sons, 1982.

Fisher, Fred. Personal Interview (Springfield, VA.). November 20, 1993.

"First Nurse Killed by Lone Rocket," *Pacific Stars & Stripes*, June 11, 1969.

Genz, Marilyn. *20,000 Men and Me*. Carpentersville, Ill.: Crossroads Communications, 1988.

Genz, Marilyn. Telephone Interview. August 30, 1994.

Hayslip, Le Ly with Jay Wurts. *When Heaven and Earth Changed Places*. New York: Penguin Books, 1990.

Hayslip, Le Ly. Letter to author. March 20, 1995

Heaton, Lt. Gen. Leonard D. Personal Letter to Mr. and Mrs. John Lane, June 10, 1969.

Hester, Col. Pauline. Personal Interview (Winston-Salem, NC). December 6, 1992.

Hines, Larry (Young). Personal Interview (Raleigh, North Carolina). September 26, 1992.

Hope, Bob with Melville Shavelson. *Don't Shoot—It's Only Me*. G.P. Putnam's Sons, 1990.

Hovis, LCDR Bobbi. *Station Hospital Saigon: A Navy Nurse in Vietnam, 1963–64*. Annapolis: United States Naval Institute, 1991.

Kane, Joseph Nathan. *Facts About the Presidents: From George Washington to Ronald Reagan*. New York: The H.W. Wilson, Co., 1981.

Kowal, Patricia. "Reflections on Operation Homecoming," *Aviation, Space, and Environmental Medicine*, Dec., 1990, pp. 1156–1158.

Kowal, Patricia. Telephone Interview. March 9, 1995.

Lane, Kay. Personal Interview (Canton, Ohio). October 10, 1992.

Lane, Sharon. Eight Letters from Fort Sam Houston, Texas, April 25, 1968–June 14, 1968.

Lane, Sharon. Thirty-one Letters from Fitzsimons Hospital, Denver, Colorado, June 18, 1968–April 1, 1969.

Lane, Sharon. Fourteen Letters from Chu Lai, RVN, April 29, 1969–June 4, 1969.

Lane, Sharon. Personal Letter to Doris Plastow, Nov. 6, 1961.

Lanning, Michael Lee and Dan Cragg. *Inside the VC and the NVA: The Real Story of North Vietnam's Armed Forces*. New York: Fawcett Columbine Book, 1992.

Lazar, Amy. Telephone Interview. September 21, 1993

Lazar, Amy. "My Year in Vietnam: Vietnam Log of Amy Lazar." Unpublished manuscript: February 2, 1969–February 2, 1970.

Lee, Kathy. Personal Letter to Mrs. Kay Lane. January 26, 1989.

Lomperis, Timothy. *The War Everyone Lost—and Won: America's Intervention in Viet Nam's Twin Struggles.* Washington, D.C.: Congressional Quarterly, 1984.

Lutz, Sylvia (Holland). Personal Diary. June 8, 1969.

Lutz, Sylvia (Holland). Telephone Interview. February 3, 1994.

Maclear, Michael. *The Ten Thousand Day War: Vietnam 1945–1975.* New York: Avon Books, 1981.

Medlin, Col. Jack. Personal Interview (Winston-Salem, N.C.). December 6, 1992; May 23, 1993.

Menton, Leta. Telephone Interview. December 2, 1993.

Menton, Leta. Personal Interview (Wheaton, Md.). December 7, 1993.

Morden, Bettie. *The Women's Army Corps: 1945–1978.* Washington, D.C.: Government Printing Office, 1990.

Neel, Maj. Gen. Spurgeon. *Medical Support of US Army in Vietnam 1965–1970: Buildup of Hospitals.* Washington, D.C.: Department of the Army, 1973.

Nixon, Richard M. Personal letter to Mr. And Mrs. John Lane, June 19, 1969.

Nixon, Richard M. *RN: The Memoirs of Richard Nixon.* New York: Grosset and Dunlap, 1978.

Norman, Elizabeth M. *Women at War: The Story of Fifty Military Nurses Who Served in Vietnam.* Philadelphia: University of Pennsylvania Press, 1990.

Obituary for Lt. Sharon A. Lane, *Newsweek*, June 23, 1969.

The Ohio Almanac. ed. by Damaine Vonada. Wilmington: Orange Frazer Press, Inc., 1992.

Office of the Adjutant General, HQ U.S. Army. Report of Casualty, June 10, 1969.

Office of the Surgeon General, U.S. Army Technical Liaison Office. "Army Loses Doctor and Two Nurses in Vietnam," News Release, February 28, 1966.

Office of the Surgeon General, U.S. Army Technical Liaison Office. "First Nurse Killed in Action in Vietnam," News Release, June 13, 1969.

Pathe, Barbara. Personal Letter to Author, September 23, 1992.

Powell, General Colin L. Personal Letter to Author. January 12, 1996.

Pratt, Col. Henry J., "Heroines of Healing," *The Retired Officer* Magazine, Nov. 1993, pp. 28–32.

Public Papers of the Presidents of the United States: Gerald R. Ford: Containing the Public Messages, Speeches, and Statements of the President, 1975. Book 1. Washington, D.C.: GPO, 1977.

Pyle, David V. "Of the nurses . . . last U.S. Servicewoman killed in the war," *Vietnam* Magazine, April 1995, pp.10, 12.

Reisman, W. Michael and Chris T. Antoniou eds. *The Laws of War: A Comprehensive Collection of Primary Documents on International Laws Governing Armed Conflict.* New York: Random House, 1994.

Robinson, Daniel and Joe Cummings. Vietnam, Laos, and Cambodia. Berkeley: Lonely Planet Publications, Inc., 1991.

Rosenfeld, Megan. "The Angels of Vietnam," *Washington Post.* Nov. 11, 1993, C-1, C-12.

Sample, Cannon. Telephone Interview. June 9, 1993.

Sheets, Doris (Plastow). Personal Interview (Canton, Ohio). April 10, 1993.

Shulimson, John and Maj. Charles M. Johnson. *U.S. Marines in Vietnam: The Landing and the Build Up, 1965.* Washington, D.C.: History and Museums Division, HQ United States Marine Corps, 1978.

Smith, Bill. Personal Interview (Palaskala, Ohio). August 23, 1993.

Smith, Mary (Mentzger). Personal Interview (Palaskala, Ohio). August 23, 1993.

Smith, Winnie. *American Daughter Gone to War.* New York: William Morrow and Company, Inc., 1992.

Spector, Ronald H. *After Tet: The Bloodiest Year in Vietnam.* New York: The Free Press, 1993.

Spelts, Doreen. "Nurses Who Served—And Did Not Return," American Journal of Nursing, September, 1986, pp. 1037–1038.

"A Statue for Sharon: Memorial Planned for Nurse Killed in Vietnam," Canton *Repository*, June 12, 1971.

Tam Ky and Points North and South. Freedom Hill Films, 1991.

"Toward the Final Agony," *Time.* June 14, 1975, pp. 8–15.

Tregaskis, Richard. *Southeast Asia, Building the Bases: The History of Construction in Southeast Asia.* Washington, D.C.: GPO, 1975.

U.S. Congress. House of Representatives. Special Subcommittee on Investigations. *The Vietnam-Cambodia Emergency, 1975 Part III—Vietnam Evacuation: Testimony of Ambassador Graham A. Martin.* 94th Congress, 2nd Session. Washington, D.C.: GPO, 1976.

U.S. Congress. Senate. Subcommittee to Investigate Problems Connected with Refugees and Escapees. *Indochina Evacuation and Refugee Problems, Part IV.* 94th Congress, 1st Session. Washington, D.C.: GPO, 1975.

Van Devanter, Lynda. *Home Before Morning.* New York: Warner Books, 1983.

VC/NVA Rocket Artillery, HQ, Armed Forces of R.V.N., Office of Joint General Staff, Oct. 18, 1967.

Vien, General Cao Van. *The Final Collapse.* Washington, D.C.: GPO, 1985.

Vietnam: A Country Study. Federal Research Division of the Library of Congress. Washington, D.C.: GPO, 1989.

"Ward 6," *Time.* 7 June 1968, p. 39.

Watts, Holly, et al. "Women in Vietnam." Hosted by Dr. Sidney Bland, James Madison University, Harrisonburg, Virginia. April 26, 1994.

Welch, Capt. Clyde E., Report of Damages Sustained During Rocket Attack to the Commanding Officer of the 44th Medical Battalion, June 10, 1969.

West, Ltc. Iris J. "The Women of the Army Nurse Corps During the Vietnam War," *Celebration of Patriotism and Courage.* Washington, D.C.: Vietnam Women's Memorial Project, pp. 35–39

Williams, William Appleton, Thomas McCormick, *et al.* eds. *American In Vietnam: A Documentary History.* New York: Anchor Books, 1985.

Wilson, James R. *Landing Zones: Southern Veterans Remember Vietnam.* Durham: Duke University Press, 1990.

INDEX